100 NUMBER GAMES

0 to 3

Easy-to-play games

Supporting first learning

DR HANNAH MORTIMER

CREDITS

British Library Cataloguing-in-Publication Data A catalogue record for this book is available from the British Library.

ISBN 0 439 98476 9

Author
Dr Hannah Mortimer

Illustrations
Gaynor Berry

Editor
Saveria Mezzana

Assistant Editor
Victoria Lee

Series Designer
Anna Oliwa

Designer
Anna Oliwa

Text © 2003 Hannah Mortimer
© 2003 Scholastic Ltd

Designed using Adobe PageMaker

Published by Scholastic Ltd,
Villiers House,
Clarendon Avenue,
Leamington Spa,
Warwickshire CV32 5PR

Visit our website at www.scholastic.co.uk
Printed by Belmont Press
1 2 3 4 5 6 7 8 9 0   3 4 5 6 7 8 9 0 1 2

Acknowledgements

The publishers gratefully acknowledge permission to reproduce the following copyright material:

© **Derek Cooknell:** p5, p6, p7, p8, p9, p10, p12, p16, p17, p19, p21, p23, p24, p25, p28, p29, p32, p35, p40, p44, p47, p52, p53, p60, p64, p69, p71, p77, p84, p86, p90, p95, p97, p101, p102, p103, p104, p110, p111, p119, p120

© **Corbis:** p59, p83

© **Eyewire:** p6, p68, p112

© **Photodisc:** p68, p98

© **Dan Howell/SODA:** p38, p54, p67

© **Ken Kaup/SODA:** p10

© **James Levin/SODA:** p38

© **Dan Powell/SODA:** p37, p54, p84

Every effort has been made to trace copyright holders and the publishers apologise for any inadvertent omissions.

CONTENTS

CHAPTER 1

CHAPTER 2

CHAPTER 3

CHAPTER 4

CONTENTS

CHAPTER 5

CHAPTER 6

CHAPTER 7

CHAPTER 8

INTRODUCTION

Early learning in number can be creative and play-centred, yet parents and carers sometimes find it hard to imagine what it could involve for a very young child who cannot yet count or read numbers. This book provides you with a range of suggestions for practical games and ideas that will inspire you to support your child's learning in a flexible and confidence-inspiring way.

How early number skills develop

The new baby is learning how to make sense of his world, taking in the sounds, shapes, movements, colours and feelings that are all around him. At first, these are a buzzing confusion of sensations and your baby does not yet have any sense of how they are linked together or even that he is a little person in his own right. Yet he has been born almost pre-programmed to learn and will actively be seeking out sounds, sights and touch as the weeks go by.

For example, he begins to learn that the sound of the door in the morning means that you are coming into the room, and so he turns to look; that the fist waving in front of his eyes belongs to him and he can move it at will; that he can knock his play centre and it makes a sound that he can then repeat; that if a toy disappears momentarily from view it still exists to be found again, and so many other things and events.

The ability to learn that toys and people continue to exist even when your child cannot see them is called 'object permanence' and is a vital early stage to understanding quantity and number. In essence, your baby is counting 'one'. He can either count 'one' of you standing over him, or he cannot and he therefore looks for you. This is why many of the early number games in this book use 'Peep-bo' and other hiding games to develop early object permanence.

Learning through play

You can start to encourage your baby to develop an interest in numbers from a very early age. Young children learn best through playing and through interactions and games with people and objects around them. Play that is best for development is play that is at just the right

developmental level for your child, or even that slightly stretches her. If you can provide the right opportunities and materials and be supportive and encouraging, you will help your child to become a successful learner.

At the beginning of each chapter, there are ideas to help you to understand the developmental stages that children go through as they develop their understanding of number and quantity. Early counting does not begin by teaching 'one, two, three' – there are many early building blocks to number that you will need to introduce first. So this book will help you to 'think developmentally', support your child's early learning of number in the most effective way, and make your learning games as interesting, successful and effective as possible.

Learning through interaction

In this book, you will find ideas for using your games and play not only to teach early number but to build a confident and positive relationship between you and your child. The best ways to do this are to tune into how your child is communicating with you and to share fun and enjoyment together. Many of the games have ideas to help you to keep your language very simple. You can begin to introduce the words for numbers, shapes and positions long before your child can say them himself. You will find that you do not have to be asking him questions all the time in order to teach him about numbers, such as 'How many?'. Instead, you can use your voice as a running commentary to help him to begin to make connections, for example, 'Look! There are *one, two, three* balls left!'. Young children only take in and respond to a few words that you are saying to them. Many of the games in this book suggest that you keep your language very short and simple and that you emphasise the key words that are going to help your child to learn about early number, for example, 'There's the *big* one'.

How you can help

At the beginning of each chapter, you will find ideas for the role that you can play in encouraging your child's early learning. One of your main roles is always to be encouraging and to inspire confidence so that she begins to see numbers as interesting and fun. Many of us who feel that we are not very good with numbers had negative experiences when we were young, which led us to believe that we were weak at mathematics. This, in turn, can make us feel uneasy when faced with numbers or calculations as adults.

By using the game-like approach in this book, you will be helping your child to see herself as a successful learner where numbers are concerned.

Numbers, shapes and sets of objects are a feature of everyday life and a game-like approach can encourage children to think of them as playful rather than tedious and complex exercises.

Daily routines and experiences

One of the number skills that we acquire is the understanding of sequences of time and how events relate to one another. We learn to understand words such as 'before', 'next', 'after' and 'yesterday, today and tomorrow'. Even young children of one and two can begin to gain an appreciation of time if we provide routines that are predictable, safe and comforting. You will find that all the chapters are arranged around typical times of day in your daily routine – getting up in the morning, doing things independently, mealtimes, going out, being busy, being lively, being together and winding down at bedtime. That is why the games in this book are most suitable for parents, carers and childminders living and working in their own homes with young children. If you use the games flexibly, you will also find plenty of opportunities for involving older brothers and sisters in the games.

Using the games

Dip into the games to suit your routine and the stage that your child has reached. Although they each state the age range that they are most suitable for, be guided by your child's own enjoyment and success, and use them flexibly. Since the aim is to inspire confidence and success, always be encouraging, and simply stop the game and move on to something else if your child is not in the right mood for it that day.

Children change all the time, and you will find that games that do not suit him one day will become more interesting when he is a little older, when he has developed different interests or when he is in a different frame of mind. Try not to follow the suggestions rigidly, but adapt and develop the games as you become more familiar with the stages of early number development. This book should become a springboard for you to become a more intuitive and reflective teacher of your child if you use it flexibly and weave in your own intimate knowledge of your child and his likes and dislikes.

Early learning

You will find that the games in this book lead on to the Foundation Stage curriculum, which your child will be following when she starts at pre-school, nursery or Reception. However, the games contain different aims because children learn best by starting with a *practical* understanding of number and quantity, and later moving on to handling written numbers and sums.

When you are helping your young child to develop her understanding of number, it is especially important not to miss these early stages, and playing games together is the very best way in which you can help her to

learn. If you lay the right foundations for early learning, then later learning will follow easily and swiftly. It is not true that children who are 'ahead' in writing numbers down and doing sums early on will always be very good at mathematics later. You will never have the same opportunity again to help your child to learn through *play* and *experience*, so enjoy it while you can and be assured that you will also be laying the best foundation for later learning.

The Foundation Stage curriculum in England is divided into six Areas of Learning, and Mathematical development is one of them. Each area is divided into a number of Early Learning Goals and there are suggested Stepping Stones that children move through on their way to acquiring these Goals. The games in this book are designed so that they help your child to move towards the Stepping Stones and Early Learning Goals for Mathematical development. You will find that the games are just as helpful if you live in another country since they are also based on what we know about how young children develop and learn.

Making learning effective

The games in this book follow the same principles that early years practitioners are encouraged to follow during the Foundation Stage: that children learn best when they initiate their own ideas within a rich and stimulating environment that you have planned for them, and that they enjoy learning best when it has a purpose for them and when they feel confident and enthusiastic about what they are doing. They need to practise early skills over and over and also to extend them to take their learning even further. That is why all the games in this book have ideas for 'taking it further'.

Young children also learn best when you help them to see number positively, when you keep up their confidence and when you encourage them by playing alongside them and help them to make links in their thinking. A game-like approach with young children can achieve all these things. In other words, remember that number should not be 'serious work' – have fun with your child and enjoy the games together.

These games will help your child to get the day off to a good start and to develop an interest in numbers, learn to count by rote and develop one-to-one correspondence using anticipation, number rhymes and counting aloud. Even young babies can be introduced to early number successfully if you play games that are just right for their level of interest and understanding.

Number games do not necessarily have to contain numbers and counting – there are many early stages to number that can be built on usefully before moving on to counting. In this chapter, you will find some ideas to help you to understand what these early stages are.

LET'S GET GOING

INTERESTING NUMBERS

New babies learn how to make sense of their world and all the sensations in it, but how does your baby begin to become interested in number shapes and written numbers? Because growing babies are so interested in sounds and shapes, you can introduce him to colourful number shapes early on. Numbers are fascinating to look at and have interesting edges and contours. You can also use number rhymes in your songs from an early age so that the rhythm of the words becomes familiar and is associated with enjoyment and playing. One-year-olds will enjoy handling numbers as well and can play with the shapes of a number inset-board long before they are old enough to fit the pieces into place. By the time he is two to three years old, he is beginning to link number symbols with words and may show a delight in the birthday cards and badges, pointing out the number '2' or the number '3'.

How you can help

● Use number shapes as part of your nursery or play area, for example, number mobiles that sparkle and turn, numbers on wall charts and posters, early picture books with simple numbers and sets of objects to count. Even before your baby is ready to do this himself, you can be counting and playing with numbers, making them an enjoyable experience.

● Do not expect your toddler to look at written numbers and name them until he shows a genuine interest. You do not want to associate numbers with difficulty and challenge before your child is ready. Avoid direct questions such as, 'How many are there?' or 'What's this number?'; instead, talk about number naturally, emphasising key words, for example, 'I wonder *how many* – shall we *count* them together?' or, 'Oh look! Can you see the number *one*? Jamie is *one* as well!'.

● As soon as your child begins to recognise certain numbers, such as 1, 2 or 3, spend time looking out for these numbers in packaging, door signs and everyday situations.

● Start by introducing numbers 1 to 3, then build up to 5 when your child is ready. Do not try to move too quickly – there is time enough to build on these early stages.

EARLY COUNTING

Your baby will probably have become familiar with hearing you count long before she has a go herself. She has to learn how to make speech sounds and to master early words before she can say the numbers to you. However, you can introduce the rhyme and rhythm of counting from an early age by building this into your daily routines, songs and rhymes. This chapter provides plenty of ideas and activities for doing this.

The first counting will probably come as part of a well-rehearsed phrase that your baby associates with pleasure. This might be your playful 'One, two, three...!' leading into a swing or a cuddle. If you do this often enough, you may find your baby echoing the vowel sounds 'u – oo – ee' (for 'one – two – three') even before her words are clear. You may then hear her add a final number to your count: 'eeeee!' after you have started 'one – two...'.

How you can help
● Count naturally through the day, for example, 'One sock on, two socks on', 'One step, two steps' and so on.
● Introduce number rhymes and chants from an early age so that your child becomes familiar with hearing the rhythm of the counting words.
● Start with a simple 'one, two, three' phrase and later build up to five and then ten.
● Count out plates, cups, spoons as you lay them on the table together.
● When she begins to join in with you, leave out alternate words for her to fill in, for example, 'One... (two)... three... (four)...'.

ONE-TO-ONE CORRESPONDENCE

The ability to link one counting number with one object is called developing 'one-to-one correspondence'. At first, you may find that your child can count 'by rote'. That means that he can remember a string of numbers and recite them 'one, two, three, four, five'. However, when you place five bricks in front of him, he is most likely to touch the first brick and finish chanting his 'one, two, three, four, five' long before he touches the last brick. He has not yet learned to touch one and count one and this is a normal step in his development. He now knows that touching and counting can go together – in other words, he has grasped the idea that *quantity* can be counted and numbered.

In time, he will learn to count the bricks methodically, saying one number for each brick that he

touches. He has now developed 'one-to-one correspondence'. Typically, children count by rote to about ten before they begin to count objects to four or five, so it is a skill that slightly follows the ability to count by rote.

How you can help
● Play games that involve counting by rote before you start counting out objects.
● Make sure that your games include both 'give' and 'take', saying, for example, 'Give me two cars' and, 'Here is one tractor'.
● Start with low numbers of objects to be counted out, for example, three to begin with, building up to five and then more.
● Guide your child's finger to touch as he counts.
● Help your child to arrange objects in a line before counting them out, moving from left to right.
● Count the stairs out loud as you go up and down.
● Count out things that you see together when you are out, always starting from 'one' at first, saying, for example, 'Look! One cow, two cows!' rather than, 'Look! Two cows!'.

AGE RANGE
0–1 year

LEARNING
OPPORTUNITIES
● To enjoy water play
● To repeat actions
● To link cause with
effect
● To enjoy numbers.

YOU WILL NEED
Your usual baby bath
equipment.

Splish, splosh!

Sharing the game

● Play this game during a morning or evening bathtime, or take the bath outdoors on a warm sunny day.
● This game is best for babies of four to nine months.
● Support your baby in a semi-reclining position in the water so that she feels safe and secure.
● Lean where she can see you clearly, and gently splash the water saying, 'Splish!'.
● Encourage her to repeat the action, moving her hand gently if you need to. Say, 'Splosh!' as she repeats the gentle splash.
● Now enjoy a gentle splashing game as you chant this rhyme to her:
  Splish! Splosh! One! Two!
  (Your baby's name) is having a splash now!
  Splishing her toes and sploshing her nose –
  (Your baby's name) is having a bath now!
  Hannah Mortimer

● Splash water over her toes, then touch her gently on the nose with your wet finger as you reach the third line.
● You can repeat the rhyme with her at drying time:
  Rub! Dub! One! Two!
  (Your baby's name) is having a dry now!
  Rubbing her toes and rubbing her nose –
  (Your baby's name) is having a dry now!
  Hannah Mortimer
● If you enjoy singing, you can use the tune of the traditional nursery rhyme, 'See-Saw, Marjory Daw'.

Taking it further

● Introduce more body parts – it does not really matter if they do not rhyme or scan!
● Pause between splashes to allow her to copy all by herself.

LEARNING OPPORTUNITIES
● To link cause with effect
● To repeat one sound
● To shake, rattle and bang.

YOU WILL NEED
A hand-held rattle or shaker.

Copycats

Sharing the game

● This game makes a useful distraction at nappy-changing time. Try it first thing in the morning to get you both going!

● It is best for babies who have just begun to hold a rattle and to shake it and who are also at the stage of passing toys to you and then taking them back from you again.

● When your baby is lying on his back on the changing mat, offer a rattle for him to hold.

● Allow him a moment or two to examine it, to mouth it, to drop it or to pass it between his hands – all these are clever baby skills!

● Hold out your hand and say 'thank you' as he hands you the rattle. Say, 'My turn!' as you give it a good shake.

● Offer it back to your baby. Say, '*(Your baby's name)*'s turn!' and move your hand gently over his to shake it again.

● Repeat a few times, playing a 'My turn-your turn' game, helping your baby each time if you need to.

Taking it further

● After a few games, your baby may begin to shake the rattle when it is his turn. Celebrate with a cheer and a cuddle.

● Try to think of other games that you can play, for example, copying each other on a drum, or clicking two bricks together.

● Play an echoing game. When your child makes a babbling noise, echo it gently back to him and then remember to give him a smile or a cuddle afterwards.

AGE RANGE
0–1 year

LEARNING OPPORTUNITIES
● To anticipate
● To develop eye contact
● To enjoy numbers.

YOU WILL NEED
A duvet; rug; cushions.

More, please!

Sharing the game

● This makes a lovely gentle start to a day. Spread the duvet on the carpet or on top of a rug outside.

● Lie your baby on the duvet or prop her up with the cushions.

● Spend a few moments making sounds to each other and smiling together. Encourage eye contact by moving your head into your baby's line of vision.

● If your baby is in a chuckling mood, give her a little tickle to make her laugh, and develop this into a game. Take care not to startle a young baby – this game is best from about age three months.

● Say, 'One, two, three… *tickle* the baby!' using your voice intonation and pausing before the word 'tickle' to build up the excitement and fun for your baby.

● After a few turns, older babies will begin to move and gurgle in anticipation of what you are about to do.

● If your baby has reached this stage, you can pause after each turn and say, 'More?', waiting for her anticipation before you repeat the tickling game.

Taking it further

● Look for other natural opportunities to use the question, 'More?', for example, when you push the buggy quickly or offer a spoonful of breakfast.

● Use 'More?' between verses of 'Round and Round the Garden' (Traditional) or other tickling and cuddling rhymes.

AGE RANGE
0–1 year

LEARNING OPPORTUNITIES
● To develop awareness of shape
● To explore by feeling
● To listen to counting.

YOU WILL NEED
A selection of light-weight packaging in different shapes, such as empty talcum-powder drums, little boxes, small empty plastic bottles, empty triangular chocolate tubes, and so on; basket; brightly coloured wrapping paper; sticky tape; your usual changing mat and nappy-changing equipment.

THINK FIRST!
Stay with your baby throughout this game so that you can check that he does not chew or swallow any loose materials. Remove any small tops or parts that he might loosen and swallow.

Feeling in shape

Sharing the game
● Wrap some of the boxes using the wrapping paper and sticky tape.
● Collect your different shapes in a basket and keep it near to the changing mat.
● When it is nappy-changing time, place your baby on the changing mat. Choose a shape from your basket, pass it to him and say, 'One for you!'. Talk softly as he handles it and mouths it.
● After a while (or if the package is becoming chewed!), offer the next shape. Your baby will probably drop or release the first.
● Again, give him time to look at it and feel it before offering the next shape.
● In this way, you may be able to keep him interested, alert and distracted during changing time and introduce him to early counting and shapes as well.

Taking it further
● Older babies will be able to hold two objects at once. Say, 'One for you… two for you!' as you pass them to your baby.
● Add new and different shapes to your basket to keep the novelty and interest going.

LET'S GET GOING

AGE RANGE
1–2 years

LEARNING OPPORTUNITIES
● To develop manipulation skills
● To develop awareness of numbers.

YOU WILL NEED
A teddy bear with a coat (or you can make your own bear's coat out of baby clothes or felt); needle and thread for yourself; three large cardigan buttons; sticky labels that are the same shape and size as the buttons; pen.

Teddy's coat

Sharing the game
● Fit Bear up with a simple coat that opens easily at the front.
● Sew on three large cardigan buttons and make sure that the button holes are wide and loose enough to take them.
● Stick a label over each button. Write '1' on the top button, '2' on the middle button and '3' on the bottom button.
● Try this game when

you are dressing your toddler in the morning. Help her to button and unbutton Bear's coat and chant, 'One, two, three!' as you button it up, one button at a time, popping it through the hole and inviting your toddler to grasp each button in turn and pull it through as you count the number.
● Enjoy touching each of the buttons in turn and chanting the numbers together.
● Count out any buttons on your own clothing or your child's clothing for her to watch and listen to.

Taking it further
● Your older child will be able to do the buttoning and unbuttoning without help.
● With your older child, make comments such as, 'Bear's hot! Can you undo button number 1?' or, 'Oh look! Number 2 has come undone!', challenging her to recognise specific numbers on the buttons.
● Always count buttons and fastenings as you do them up or undo them for your child, for example, saying, 'One strap… two straps!'.

○●○●○●○●○●○●○●○●○●○●○●○●○●○●○●○

LEARNING OPPORTUNITIES
● To count one to two
● To develop object permanence.

YOU WILL NEED
A favourite soft toy, such as a rabbit or teddy bear; pillows or cushions; covers.

Where's Teddy?

Sharing the game

● Settle down with your toddler on a carpet or floor, for example, in the bedroom when you are getting up. Scatter cushions and covers around you on the floor or bed.
● Pick up Teddy (or which ever soft toy you have chosen for the game) and move it around to attract your toddler's attention. Make it dance and squeak.
● Now say, 'Hide Teddy!' as you swoop it underneath one of the cushions or covers. Continue to hold on to it as you chant, 'One… two… *Here's* Teddy!' and make it reappear again.
● Share chuckles together and give Teddy to your toddler to cuddle for a few moments.

● After several turns, invite your toddler to find Teddy when you hide it and continue to chant the words.
● When you are both familiar with the game, encourage your toddler to hide Teddy. Lift a cushion or cover and help him if necessary.
● Your older child might begin to say the counting words 'one, two', or even join in with the 'two' once you have said the 'one'.

Taking it further

● Try saying, 'One… two…' as you introduce the next spoonful of food at mealtimes.
● Find a big drum or an upturned plastic bucket and take it in turns to beat it as you chant, 'One… two…' together.

LET'S GET GOING

Babies and wash times

AGE RANGE
1–2 years

LEARNING OPPORTUNITIES
● To develop early counting
● To develop imagination
● To be aware of daily routines.

YOU WILL NEED
Three cuddly toys; dry facecloth and towel.

Sharing the game

● Play this game before you wash your toddler in the morning. Arrange three cuddly toys on a bed or carpet and tell her that it is wash time!

● Wipe each toy's face in turn as you say, 'One face, two faces, three faces!'. Invite your toddler to have a turn at wiping each toy's face as you count them again.

● Now 'dry' each face as you count, then invite your child to take a turn too.

● When you wash your toddler, use your counting again, saying, for example, 'One ear, two ears!' or, 'One hand washed, two hands washed!'.

● Count your toddler's toes as you dry them after bathtime and enjoy the rhyme 'This Little Piggy Went to Market' (Traditional) with her as you count and dry each toe in turn. Finish with a tickle.

Taking it further

● You can also play this game with plastic toys in the bath, using wet facecloths and drying off with towels.

● Fill a baby bath with lukewarm water and place it outside on a sunny day. Provide plastic dolls and toys for your child to wash. Add some bath bubbles to make this even more fun!

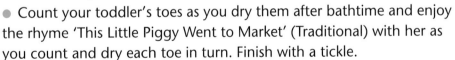

AGE RANGE
1–2 years

LEARNING OPPORTUNITIES
● To enjoy morning bathtime
● To develop an awareness of simple rocking rhythm.

YOU WILL NEED
Your usual bathtime equipment; large soft towel, warmed on a towel rail or in the airing cupboard; comfortable place to sit.

Rub-a-dub-dub

Sharing the game

● After bathtime, wrap your toddler cosily in the towel and lift him on to your lap. Bundle him in and rock him gently like a baby.
● Chant this song as you enjoy a cuddle and a rock together:
Rub-a-dub, rub-a-dub, rub-a-dub din
We've finished our bath and we're clean as a pin
We've washed all your toes and we've polished your nose
Here's a toasty warm towel to wrap *(your child's name)* in!
Hannah Mortimer

● Rub your toddler gently as you chant the first two lines. Touch his toes and his nose gently as you chant the third line and have a big cuddle in the fourth. Say your child's name in the final line of the rhyme.

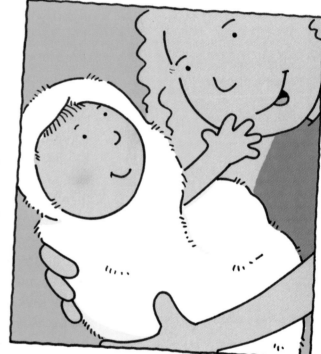

● Finish with some gentle rocks as you softly chant, 'One… two…' in time with your movements.
● This can make a gentle start to a new day, so plan the game for a time when you are not rushed. Try it as part of your regular bathtime routine.

Taking it further

● Look for other ways of playing with a 'one-two' rhythm. Count, 'One, two' as you push your child to and fro on a toddler swing, or chant, 'One, two' as you march down the path.
● Use baby oils to gently massage your toddler's toes as you count them out loud.

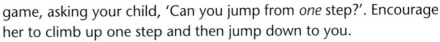

LET'S GET GOING

AGE RANGE
2–3 years

LEARNING OPPORTUNITIES
● To enjoy counting
● To become familiar with daily routines.

YOU WILL NEED
A staircase.

Down the stairs

Sharing the game

● When you are ready to go downstairs for the day, try this game with your child as part of your regular routine. If you live in a bungalow or flat, save it for next time you go down steps or stairs together.

● Stand at the top of the staircase, side by side holding hands, or one behind the other.

● As you go down the stairs, count each step that your child is on loudly and clearly: 'One, two, three, four…'.

● When you reach the bottom step, stop for a

game, asking your child, 'Can you jump from *one* step?'. Encourage her to climb up one step and then jump down to you.

● You can build this up to two or three steps if your child is a competent jumper. Be there to catch her and steady her and count with her as she climbs the steps.

● Play the counting game as you go upstairs again at the end of the day. Keep it fun so that the words become totally familiar to your child, even if she cannot count yet.

Taking it further

● Set challenges for your child outside, for example, 'Can you make *three* giant footsteps?', 'Can you jump *two* times?', 'Can you clap *one* time?' and so on.

● Your older child may be able to learn simple ordinal number. This means learning to understand words such as 'first', 'second' and 'third'. Challenge your child to stand on the *first* step or jump from the *third*.

LEARNING OPPORTUNITIES
● To enjoy number rhymes
● To feel happy at the start of the day.

YOU WILL NEED
The rhyme 'Good morning, sunshine!' on page 125; paper; washable pens.

Good morning!

Sharing the game

● Enjoy the rhyme 'Good morning, sunshine!' together as you first open the curtains or greet the day.

● Talk about the weather today. Can you see the sun?

● After breakfast, invite your child to make a picture with you. Sit at a table with the paper and pens and enjoy making huge sunshine pictures together.

● Encourage your child as he creates his picture. In the early stages, he will want to choose his own colours and make wide scribbles. When he is older, you will be able to talk together about different colours and which he would like to choose for his picture, and to encourage him to draw 'round and round' to make a circular shape.

● Recite the rhyme together as your child draws his sunshine picture, encouraging him to join in with the 'one – two – three!'.

● Stick the completed picture up in the bedroom and use it to remind yourself of the rhyme when you sing it next day.

Taking it further

● Invent a new rhyme together for 'Good evening, moonshine!'.

● Share the rhyme 'Starting the day' on page 125.

● Enjoy chasing your shadows outside on a sunny day, looking for the dark patches. Encourage your child to stand still as you draw around his shadow with chalk.

LEARNING OPPORTUNITIES
● To count to three
● To respond to 'one more', 'one less' and so on.

YOU WILL NEED
Sets of up to three objects or toys, such as three toy cars, three boots and three teddies; 'magic wand' or short colourful stick; cloth.

Magic wand

Sharing the game
● Tell your child that you are going to play a counting game. Sit down on the floor or at a low table together.
● Arrange three toy cars together, in a line, on the table or floor and count them together. Move your child's finger to help her to count if necessary.
● When you have counted them, say to your child, '*How many* cars? *Three* cars!', then ask her again, '*How many cars?*', encouraging her to complete the answer herself this time.

● Now cover the toy cars with a cloth. Slip one car away from under the cloth. Wave your 'magic wand' as you say, 'One less car!'.
● Whip the cloth away and recount the cars together. You can now use your magic wand to make three cars again, saying, 'One more car!'.
● Continue the game with different sets of objects, encouraging your child to gradually take control and become the 'magician'.
● Help her with the counting if you have to and assist your older child in beginning to predict how many toys there will be when you 'magic' one more or one less.

Taking it further
● Hide raisins under three plastic beakers – one under one, two under another and three under a third one. Challenge your child to find and eat the raisins that are under the beaker 'with two raisins'. Count them, then talk about there being 'one less' after your child has eaten one.
● Use this kind of language naturally at mealtimes, for example, 'Would you like one more?'.

AGE RANGE
2–3 years

LEARNING OPPORTUNITIES
● To enjoy number rhymes
● To join in with confidence.

YOU WILL NEED
A comfortable sofa or cushion to sit together on; paper; crayons or washable felt-tipped pens; scissors for yourself.

Five little hamsters

Sharing the game
● Sit together comfortably.
● Introduce this song to your child, sung loosely to the first two lines (repeated) of the tune 'Twinkle, Twinkle, Little Star' (Traditional):
  Five little hamsters gnawing bread,
  One fell down and bumped his head!
  Four little hamsters nibbling fruit,
  One fell down and hurt his foot!
  Three little hamsters one, two, three,
  One fell down and banged his knee!
  Two little hamsters having fun,
  One ran away and then there was one!
  One little hamster all alone,
  Called for his friends and they all went home!
Hannah Mortimer

● As you sing, use your fingers to show '5' for the first verse, reducing your fingers to '1' for the last, until all five come back at the end.
● Now move to a table and draw some hamsters on your paper together (a simple round ball with two eyes and whiskers at one end is fine!). Cut them up and use them to act out the song together.
● Make your paper hamsters disappear and reappear as you sing the rhyme, pausing to count them between verses.

Taking it further
● Many simple number rhymes can be acted out with simple props. This makes them seem more real for your child and makes the counting and understanding easier for him.
● Try using plastic bottles and singing the song 'Ten Green Bottles' together, or play with cuddly toys as you sing 'There Were Ten in the Bed' (both Traditional).

CHAPTER 2

ALL BY MYSELF

The games in this chapter use textures and materials, dressing, undressing and self-help to encourage simple comparison (which is one of the earliest number skills) and help children to use words such as 'same', 'different', 'first' and 'last'. Learning that things around them can be the same or different helps children to see that certain objects go together into sets and can be sorted, counted and matched. This ability is called 'counting sets' – a 'set' is any quantity of the same sort of thing. This chapter also provides games for children to learn about sequences of actions ('first' and 'last'), which help them to understand the passage of time and how events in the world relate together.

HANDLING AND EXPLORING

The earliest stage of making comparisons will emerge out of your baby's ability to see, touch and explore his world. Long before he has the language or understanding to tell you that things are the 'same' or 'different', he will explore, touching, swiping, feeling and mouthing anything with which his hands come into contact. Dressing and undressing times provide ideal opportunities for exploring different textures and materials. It is only after your child has had chances to link together what he sees, touches and feels that he can begin to make sense of which things in his world go together into sets or 'concepts'. He is already becoming a little scientist, working out what he must do to move his body in order to explore his surroundings – how to swipe his arms to jiggle the mobile, or how to reach and grasp to secure the rattle. This early stage of exploration is called 'an understanding of cause and effect'.

How you can help
● At changing and dressing times, allow time for your baby to enjoy the feelings and textures around him. Give him something to hold and feel as you are dressing him, and talk gently and soothingly.
● Provide opportunities for your child to explore with bare feet as well as hands. Textures and fabrics can be lovely to lie and kick on as well.

● Accept the fact that your baby is mouthing everything – this is all part of his method of exploring. Keep an eye open for loose items that could be swallowed or choked on, and be mindful of cleanliness and hygiene.

MAKING SIMPLE COMPARISONS

Once your child has enjoyed playing and exploring, she will begin to make simple comparisons. You might notice her placing two yellow bricks together, or picking up two teddy bears at once. First of all, you will see her match similar things together, then she will be able to sort (for example, placing all the toy cars in

When your child is older, play games sorting the socks into pairs, the spoons from the forks, finding cups and saucers that go together, and so on. Toy tea services in primary colours give good opportunities for matching colours and developing one-to-one correspondence.

With your older child, look for opportunities to introduce the words for opposites and differences, for example, 'Look! That's *full*!… Now it's *empty*!'.

Enjoy emptying and filling games together as you explore how quantities change and differ.

on to another – which is another vital aspect to learning how to handle words, numbers and language later on.

How you can help

- Start by introducing the words 'first' and 'last' into your daily conversations in natural situations.
- Move on to introducing 'second' and 'third', perhaps using a game, such as playing with cars or doing up buttons.
- Climbing up and down stairs together also provides opportunities for counting together and talking about ordinal numbers.
- Higher ordinal numbers tend to be mastered a little later – when your child is at nursery or pre-school.

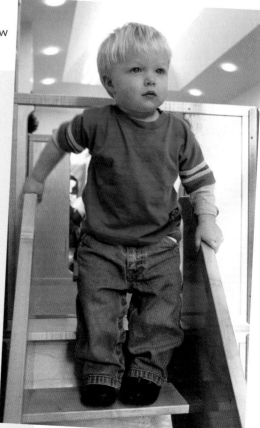

one box and all the toy people in another), then identify (handing you the red one when you ask, 'Which is the red one?') and later name ('That's a cow!' or 'That's blue!'). If you can remember this sequence – match, sort, identify, name – it will help you to make your games easier or harder depending on the stage that your child has reached. Typically, she will match objects first (for example, placing cups together or collecting cars in her hands), then photographs to things (such as matching a photo of Grandma to Grandma herself), then pictures to objects (matching a drawing of a dog to the real dog), then colours (placing red bricks into a red box), then sizes (matching big balls or little balls), then more complex characteristics, such as 'long'/'short', 'high'/'low', 'full'/'empty' and 'heavy'/'light'.

How you can help

- Draw your child's attention to sameness, saying, for example, 'Here's another glove!' or 'There's a shoe, too!'.

FIRST AND LAST

Another kind of comparison that your child will learn to make is the one between 'first' and 'last'. Position numbers, such as 'first', 'second' and 'third', are 'ordinal numbers'. Typically, your child will learn to count by rote ('one, two, three') before he will understand or use ordinal numbers. However, he can be exposed to these if you introduce them into your daily language, for example, '*Last* sock!', 'You're *first*!' and so on. Dressing and undressing times also provide plenty of opportunity for talking about the order in which things happen. Your child will be able to learn about sequences – how one thing usually leads

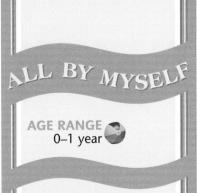
LEARNING OPPORTUNITIES
● To notice sameness
● To anticipate numbers
● To co-operate during dressing.

YOU WILL NEED
A pair of baby socks, shoes or boots.

One, two, put on my shoe

Sharing the game
● This game is best played when you are dressing your baby, though it adapts easily to taking clothes off as well.
● Hold up her socks, shoes or boots and bring each one into sight in turn, saying, 'One sock, two socks!' (or shoe or boot).
● As you put them on to your baby's feet, count them once more: 'One sock, two socks!'.
● Finally, hold each sock in turn as you jiggle the foot and say, 'All done! One sock, two socks!'.
● For your older child, pop one sock on, then look together for the second one. Again, count as you find each one.

Taking it further
● Scatter a few socks or shoes around the floor. Place one on to your baby's foot, then hold up others beside it as you look for the matching one. As you try this, say, 'Same? No!' or, 'Same? Yes!' as you make the comparisons.
● Challenge your older baby with, 'Where's your shoe?' and encourage her to look around for it.
● You can also play a game of pairing shoes or socks together, drawing your baby's attention to the way they look by saying, 'Look! The same!'.

LEARNING OPPORTUNITIES
● To develop object permanence
● To be aware of different sizes
● To anticipate.

YOU WILL NEED
Light silk and chiffon scarves in different colours and sizes.

Peep-bo!

Sharing the game

● Wait until your baby is wide awake and enjoying a chuckle with you. This game is best for babies of about three to nine months.
● Sit your baby in his car seat or bouncy cradle. Move close to him and smile and make soft sounds to each other.
● Place one of the scarves over your own head, then immediately pull it off saying, 'Boo!'.
● Repeat this a few times so that it develops into a game. Keep the turns short so that your baby continues to look in your direction.
● Now lightly place a scarf over your baby's face, then draw it away saying, 'Boo!'. Again, repeat this a few times so that it develops into a game. Share pleasure and laughter as you miraculously 'reappear'!
● For an older baby, leave the scarf lightly on his face and see whether he begins to pull it off himself. He will delight in pulling the scarf to one side so that he can share your laughter as you say, 'Boo!'.
● Enjoy exploring different colours, sizes and textures by using many different scarves. Try small squares of silk and larger shawls, too.

Taking it further
● Bob down out of view and then reappear with a 'Boo!'.
● Place a favourite toy momentarily behind a cushion, then make it reappear. Encourage your older baby to search for the lost toy by looking or even by pulling at the cushion.

**LEARNING
OPPORTUNITIES**
● To link cause and effect
● To enjoy social contact
● To involve siblings.

YOU WILL NEED
A quiet place to be
comfortable together.

Tickle toes

Sharing the game

● This is a number rhyme for the times of day when you are dressing, undressing, bathing or changing your baby.

● Look for a quiet area where you can enjoy each other's company for a short while.

● As you reach bare toes, gently wiggle each toe in turn, first on one foot and then on the other, as you say the following counting rhyme:

One, two, three, four, five little toes;
Wiggle them, jiggle them, tickle each toe!
One, two, three, four, five more little toes;
Wiggle them, jiggle them, tickle them, so!
Hannah Mortimer

● You can also adapt this rhyme for any time of day by substituting 'fingers' for 'toes'.

● If you have an older child, this might be a lovely way to involve her at changing or dressing times. Chant the rhyme together as your older child gently touches the fingers or toes. An older child feels important and valued if the baby enjoys what they are doing and this helps to build their relationship.

● You can also adapt the game to include other body parts and chant as you are washing or drying your baby:

One little nose and two little ears;
Wiggle them, jiggle them, tickle each one! *(and so on).*

● Keep the tickling gentle and take the rhyme at the right pace to keep your baby happy and yet still relaxed. This 'tuning in' to the pace of your baby is an excellent way of building your relationship together.

Taking it further

● Try to involve older brothers and sisters at changing and dressing times by asking them to fetch a nappy or to help directly. Praise them warmly and tell them how much the baby likes them.

AGE RANGE
0–1 year

LEARNING OPPORTUNITIES
● To practise dressing and undressing skills
● To become familiar with counting 'my turn, your turn'.

YOU WILL NEED
A soft, floppy hat; headsquare or scarf.

Hats off!

Sharing the game
● This game is best played with older babies (eight months plus).
● Engage your baby's attention, then put the headsquare over your face and withdraw it with a 'Boo!'.
● Place it lightly over your baby's face and encourage him to pull it off himself as you say, 'Boo!'.
● Finally, place it over your face and see if you can invite him to pull it off your face so that you can 'Boo!' him again.
● Now move on to your hat. Place it on your head and make smiley faces at your baby to keep his attention.
● Then pull the hat off and place it on his head – it will probably be large enough to cover his eyes!
● Encourage him as he pulls the hat off his head and celebrate his success – he has now started to undress himself!

● Play these games with a 'my turn, your turn' rhythm – this will help your baby to anticipate what is going to happen next and help him learn to 'count' turns.

Taking it further
● See if you can encourage your baby to tug his socks off if you pull them on to the end of his feet when he is lying on his back. Let him play with them for a while afterwards.
● Let your baby handle the clothes and explore the textures as you dress and undress him. If his hands and mind are busy, this will keep him distracted while you finish what needs doing.

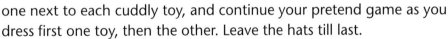

ALL BY MYSELF

AGE RANGE
1–2 years

LEARNING OPPORTUNITIES
● To develop awareness of quantity
● To make comparisons
● To practise dressing skills.

YOU WILL NEED
Two cuddly toys; dolls' or baby clothes to dress the toys in, including hats.

Wake-up call

Sharing the game
● If family life is not too rushed, play this game at the beginning of the day when you are all getting ready. Your younger child will probably watch you, and your older child will begin to join in if you make suggestions.

● Start with the cuddly toys in bed. Call, for example, 'Wake up Bear, wake up Lion – it's time to get up!'. Get the toys out of bed together and pretend to give them a wash.

● Lay out two sets of dolls' or baby clothes, one next to each cuddly toy, and continue your pretend game as you dress first one toy, then the other. Leave the hats till last.

● Draw your toddler's attention to the first toy by saying, 'Look! No hat!'. Show her the hat and see if she will pass it to you. Make a display of popping it on to the toy's head.

● Next, encourage her to pass you the second hat. Pop it on the second toy's head together and count, '*One* hat, *two* hats' for her.

Taking it further
● Your older toddler will be able to help you to find two hats for two cuddly toys, or three hats for three dolls. Help her to match these one-to-one.

● As you dress and undress your toddler, provide just as much help as is needed and encourage her to complete part of the task independently – such as pushing a foot through a trouser leg or raising her arms when you put her top on.

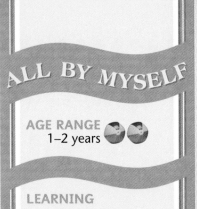

AGE RANGE
1–2 years

LEARNING OPPORTUNITIES
● To develop early counting skills
● To co-operate when having hands washed
● To make simple comparisons.

YOU WILL NEED
The poem 'Dandy handy' on page 126.

Dirty... clean!

Sharing the game
● Learn the poem or stick it on to a wall above your washbasin so that you can read it to your toddler.
● Play this game as you wash hands together in order to make hand-washing enjoyable for both you and your child.
● If his hands are very dirty, wash one hand first as you say the rhyme and count the fingers, then draw your toddler's

attention to the clean hand and the dirty hand by saying, 'Look! One clean, one dirty!'.
● As you chant the counting rhyme to your toddler, touch each finger as you count it.
● Encourage your toddler to dabble and rinse his hands to remove the soap. He will also enjoy pulling the plug out at the end. By encouraging these tiny steps in independence, you are helping your child to learn useful, new self-help skills.
● You can draw attention in the mirror to a dirty face as well, pausing to wipe off the food or the dirt and saying to your child, 'Look! Dirty face… clean face!'.

Taking it further
● Look for opportunities to help your child to make simple comparisons in day-to-day situations. For example, point out a full cup and an empty cup. Long before he understands the words 'full' and 'empty', he will be able to make visual comparisons and reach for the cup that has the juice or milk in it.

LEARNING OPPORTUNITIES
● To develop walking skills
● To explore and compare textures.

YOU WILL NEED
A selection of soft clothing, covers and quilts in different textures and sizes; clear floor area.

Textured path

Sharing the game

● This game is most enjoyed by toddlers just beginning to walk holding hands or independently.

● Take off your and your toddler's shoes and socks.

● Lay the clothes and fabrics over the floor so that they lie fairly flat but so that all the textures, colours and fabrics overlap a little.

● Hold your toddler's hands or invite her to follow you as you walk over the different items.

● Encourage her to look at her feet and see what she is stepping on. Keep up a gentle running commentary as you walk, such as, 'Red one… furry one… *(your child's name)*'s trousers!… Oooh, soft!' and so on. Stop to enjoy the feelings and textures on your feet and toes.

● Your older toddler will enjoy a game of 'Stepping-stones', if you arrange each item slightly apart and encourage her to step from one fabric to another without walking on the floor.

● Play a game of 'Pirates' with your older toddler, where you become the crocodile and 'catch' her if she steps into the 'sea'!

Taking it further

● Invite your toddler to join you in a game where you have to gather together the items into a basket to tidy up – this will give you both the chance to explore how the textures feel when you handle them too.

● Allow your child to play a rummaging game, enjoying the feeling of an assortment of clothes or items that need ironing.

LEARNING OPPORTUNITIES
● To develop an awareness of size
● To sort by size
● To describe sizes.

YOU WILL NEED
A big and little cushion; big and little chair, such as your chair and your child's chair; big and little cups, hats, balls and so on.

Different sizes

Sharing the game
● This game is best for your older toddler (18 months plus).
● Go up to your toddler's baby chair and pretend to sit on it. Draw his attention to the joke by saying (if you are Mum), 'Mum's chair? *No!*'. Then sit on your own chair and say, 'Mum's chair? *Yes!*'.
● Encourage your toddler to sit on his own chair and point out that it is *(your child's name)*'s chair. Play a little as you both try different seats and lift him and support him as he tries yours.
● Now introduce the cushions and let your toddler watch as you try each one on each chair until you sort out which should go where. Again, say 'Mum's cushion… *(your child's name)*'s cushion!'.

● You can also play with your large cup and your toddler's small one, with a large hat for you and a small one for your toddler, or a large football for yourself and a smaller ball for him. Each time, clearly emphasise to whom the item belongs – you or your child.
● You can then begin to introduce the describing words 'big' and 'little', for example, 'Look! It's a *big* ball for Mum! A *little* ball for *(your child's name)*' and so on.

Taking it further
● Name sizes naturally as you play together, saying, for example, 'What a *big* train!'.
● Place a big and small ball in front of your toddler. Say, 'Give me the *big* one, please', and hold out your hand. If he passes the wrong one, simply help him to pick up the big one instead and cheer him, 'Yes, the *big* one!'.

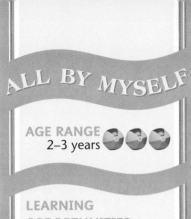
AGE RANGE
2–3 years

LEARNING OPPORTUNITIES
● To practise dressing and undressing
● To play imaginatively
● To sort clothing.

YOU WILL NEED
A suitcase; selection of spare clothes, for example, those that are too small or too big for now, or dressing-up clothes, including shoes, hats, bags, shawls, and so on.

Rainy-day case

Sharing the game
● This is a good game for a rainy day when you need something interesting to do indoors.
● Pack the suitcase ready for the next rainy day and place it somewhere out of circulation.
● When you are ready to play this game, fetch down the suitcase and help your child to lift up the lid.

● Let your child rummage and explore for a while as you watch her and add your commentary, for example, 'Yes, it was Baby's hat… Look! Grandma's shoes!'.
● Once everything is out on the floor, encourage your child to try some of the clothes on.
● This will give you more opportunities to use words such as 'big' and 'little' and to think about different sizes. Provide your child with only as much help as she needs to dress and undress.
● Now play a sorting game, putting all the shoes into the case first, then the bags.
● Look out for some new items to add to your suitcase for the next rainy day so that the contents are always a little different and new.

Taking it further
● Sort out your clothes drawers, for example, putting shoes together, jumpers together and so on.
● Match pairs of shoes, wellington boots and slippers.
● Sort out your everyday-cutlery drawer into knives, forks and spoons – take care that there is nothing sharp or too small!

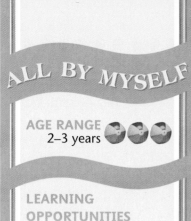
LEARNING
OPPORTUNITIES
● To grade by size
● To practise dressing
and undressing skills
● To describe size.

YOU WILL NEED
Your usual household
assortment of boots,
slippers and shoes.

Boot box

Sharing the game

● Make sure (if you
need to!) that the
footwear is untidy and
spread out before you
start this game.

● Suggest to your child
that you play a tidying
up game together.
Keep it fun so that
tidying-up seems like a
game to him.

● Play together as you
sort the footwear into
pairs. Teach your child
to make visual
comparisons by
placing one beside
another and asking him if they go together or not.

● As you play, talk about who the shoes or slippers might belong to.
Are these Grandma's? Are these Sanjay's? Where are Dad's slippers?
Introduce the words 'big' and 'little' as you talk together.

● Help your child to try on his boots, slippers and shoes to see if they
are 'just right'.

● Rearrange the footwear neatly, sorting it into boots, slippers and
shoes, or into sets that belong to the same family member.

Taking it further

● Tackle the weekly iron with your child by asking him to help you to
sort socks and different family members' clean washing!

● Sort your towels by opening them out and comparing the sizes,
then folding them neatly for your child to place in a pile, the largest
at the bottom.

● Placing 'eyes' with indelible pen on wellington boots can help your
child to sort right foot from left foot by lining up the eyes close
together before putting the boots on!

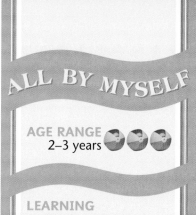

AGE RANGE
2–3 years

LEARNING OPPORTUNITIES
● To match by colour and pattern
● To practise dressing and undressing skills.

YOU WILL NEED
Ten pairs of socks in very different sizes, colours and textures.

Sock drawer

Sharing the game

● Sit down together on a carpet or mat. Spread the socks in front of you on the floor.

● Take it in turns to pick up one sock and find its match, then place the pair on one side.

● Encourage visual comparisons by placing the sock beside each of the others, asking your child if the socks are 'the same'.

● Introduce the words 'same' and 'different' as you play together.

● Now hide one of each pair of socks around the room. Challenge your child to pick up one from the floor and then hunt for the other.

● Let your child take a turn at hiding the socks for you to find too – you can make this game a lot of fun for your older child by pretending to make mistakes and allowing her to correct you!

● Now try putting the socks on and comparing them, saying whether they are the same or different.

Taking it further

● Begin to talk about matching colours in clothing, for example, 'Look! *Red* trousers, *red* top!'.

● Try to allow your child choices when dressing and undressing. You can always make the wider selection but offer your child the final choice, saying, for example, 'Do you want *this* one or *this* one?'.

LEARNING OPPORTUNITIES
● To practise dressing and undressing
● To listen carefully
● To respond to 'first' and 'next'.

YOU WILL NEED
Your child's usual selection of daily clothing.

Time and motion

Sharing the game
● Arrange your child's clothes on the bed, sofa or floor so that each is easy to pick up the right way. Put the first item to be put on to the left, and the last item to the right.
● Start from the left-hand side of your row of clothes and spend a few mornings just working out how much your child can do himself and how much help he needs with each item.
● As your child puts on each item of clothing, say, '*First* nappy, *next* vest, *next* top… *last* shoes' and move from left to right along your line of clothes.

● Once you are clear just how independent your child can be, stay close to him to offer just the right level of support – holding up a top for his arms to go in, or placing a Velcro strap into position on his shoe.
● Cheer him as he manages more and more by himself!
● Later, set a counting challenge as he puts something on by himself. Can he put his vest on all by himself while you count to three? Count slowly so that he can succeed.

Taking it further
● Your older child can be challenged to dress or undress all by himself while you time him on a clock. Give him a sticker for success or for achieving a new 'record'!
● Talk about what you will eat for tea, using sentences such as, 'What will you eat *first*?', 'What *next*?' and, 'What will you eat *last*?'.

CHAPTER 3

Games for meal and snack times help children to develop their understanding of quantity and respond to words such as 'more', 'less', 'lots' and 'all gone'. Young children learn best from familiar everyday situations, so mealtimes provide a wealth of opportunities for handling quantity and for seeing how amounts change as they eat up their food or ask for more.

MEALTIMES

MAKING SIMPLE PREDICTIONS

In the first few months, your baby is coming to terms with all the sights, sounds, feelings, smells and tastes around him. At first, these are a confusing jumble, but very quickly, they begin to make sense to him and to become predictable as well – the smell of this object that moves goes with the nice feeling of being held and then fed, making him think, 'It must be Mum!'.

As soon as he realises that objects in the world around him are stable and persist through time, he is ready to make simple predictions about his world and to anticipate what comes next. Gradually, he will become able to understand his daily routines and to realise that one thing is inevitably followed by another. That is why it is so important to provide a baby with a stable and predictable daily routine.

How you can help
● Try not to overwhelm your young baby with stimulation when he is still at the point of making sense of it all. Use gentle routines and calmness to establish confidence first. He will learn best when he is neither too aroused nor too sleepy.
● Try to always use the same voice as you get close to your baby, to help him to link the sound of your voice with your face and actions. Even tiny babies are fascinated by faces, so look at him and talk as you feed him. This will help him to co-ordinate his senses and begin to see the world as a predictable place.
● Play 'Peep-bo' and 'Hide-and-seek' games to encourage anticipation in your older baby. You can use these games to help with the final mouthfuls at mealtimes, too!
● Encourage your toddler to search for items that he has dropped, to look down as items fall from the high chair or to find something that you have hidden close by.
● Use photographs with your older child to establish memories and to remember. Enjoy magazine photographs of food and talk about what is coming next at mealtimes.

How you can help

● Provide opportunities for your child to play with sets of objects – bricks, cuddly toys, spoons, plastic cups, pieces of fruit, stacking beakers and so on. Make sure that the non-food items cannot be swallowed and that your child is not allergic to the food items.

● Provide containers, bowls and cups for your child to put things in and take out of again.

● Use mealtimes as a chance to play with quantities, and expect your child to touch and play with her food in the early stages – it is all part of learning and feeling relaxed about feeding. Be prepared for mess with a plastic sheet on the floor and plenty of bibs and wipes!

● Introduce the words 'more' and 'all gone' and use them regularly as you feed your child.

● Play with materials that change in quantity as you handle them – sand and water are useful starting-points.

UNDERSTANDING CHANGE

There is a wonderful stage around the first birthday when children suddenly begin to 'gather' objects. Your child will probably delight in picking up toys and collecting them together in containers, spending happy times emptying and filling, over and over again. At this stage, you may begin to see her combining objects together in her play, banging them together, stacking one on top of another, lining them up and so on. It suddenly becomes clear that she has the idea that certain objects can be 'the same' and can be used or collected together in some way. This stage has to come before she can begin to understand sets and quantities. You can tell from her play that she is gathering 'more' and knows when she has 'less'. The fact that she is playing with sets of objects means that she is gaining important experiences about how quantities change as she manipulates and handles them.

UNDERSTANDING QUANTITY

Before your child counts 'how many', he will probably refer to things as 'lots'. This is his first counting, since he recognises when he has just one or two and when he has plenty. You may be amused to hear him learn to count 'one, two, three, lots'! From his early games with sets of objects and quantities of food, he will begin to make judgements about quantity based on how things look – and this visual judgement will become most important when he later learns to count reliably. So understanding 'lots' is a clever number stage that he will soon pass through!

How you can help

● Introduce the word 'lots' in your everyday conversations and at your child's mealtimes.

● Play games where you pass toys or share food items between you and say things such as, 'Who has lots now?' and, 'Give me lots too!'.

● Begin to play games where you match quantities together, saying, for example, 'Give Sammy *lots*, give Teddy *lots*… Give Sammy *just one*, give Teddy *just one*'.

● Use snack times to develop early counting, for example, counting out the biscuits, pieces of fruit, slices of sausage, chips… It is a good idea to count on a regular basis long before your child does, and to make spoken numbers an enjoyable part of your daily mealtimes.

LEARNING OPPORTUNITIES
● To develop understanding of 'all gone'
● To enjoy mealtimes.

YOU WILL NEED
Your usual mealtime feeding equipment, with an extra bowl and spoon.

All gone!

Sharing the game
● This game is best played with a baby who is at the stage of learning to take food from your spoon. Use the game to hold attention and keep mealtimes fun and relaxed.
● Sit your baby in his usual high chair and organise yourself with bibs and spoons.
● Take a little of your baby's food (about three spoonfuls) into a second bowl, which you can hold up as you feed your baby.
● Spoon three mouthfuls of food to your baby, then show the bowl and say, 'All gone!'. Take a little more into your feeding bowl and continue until your baby is no longer hungry.

● As you feed him, place a second spoon in his hand so that he can get used to the feel of it.
● When your baby is a bit older, place a little food into a dish for him to 'play with' as you feed him still. This is all part of the experience of learning to feed himself!
● Teach finger-feeding by putting a dab of a favourite food on to his fingers for him to lick. Again, say, 'All gone!' as he licks it clean.

Taking it further
● Use 'All gone!' whenever it is appropriate throughout the day, for example, when brothers or sisters have gone out to play, when the television is switched off, when all the milk is drunk, and so on.
● Introduce another mealtime word to your baby after you have said, 'All gone!', asking him, 'More?'.

LEARNING OPPORTUNITIES
● To develop feeding skills
● To be aware of quantity.

YOU WILL NEED
Your usual mealtime spoon, bowl and mashed food, with an extra spoon.

Spoon full

Sharing the game

● This game is helpful to play when your baby is just beginning to show an interest in lifting a spoon to her mouth herself.

● Before you reach that stage, give her a second spoon to play with as you feed her. You will notice that she reaches a point where she starts putting the spoon into the food, even though she is not able to load it up just yet.

● Choose sticky food that stays on her spoon even when she twists her hand.

● Load one of the spoons up with a little bit

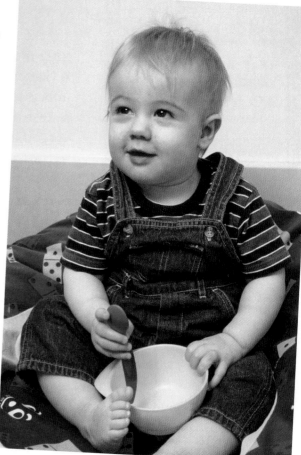

of food and place it in her hand. Encourage her as she lifts it to her mouth. Load the other spoon as she is eating.

● After a time, you will be able to load the spoon and then leave it on the side of her bowl for her to pick up and lift to her mouth herself. She is now nearly feeding herself!

Taking it further

● Breaking an activity down into easy steps and encouraging your baby gradually is a useful way of helping development. Think of other occasions when you can use this approach, for example, when you teach her to pull off a sock, with you starting it off for her and then encouraging her to do more and more by herself.

LEARNING OPPORTUNITIES
● To anticipate numbers
● To develop feeding skills.

YOU WILL NEED
Your usual mealtime feeding equipment.

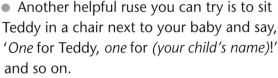

Chuffer train

Sharing the game
● This game is most suitable if your child is learning to eat from a spoon. Use it when his appetite is flagging a little towards the end of the meal.
● Make your spoon into a 'chuffer train'. Make it 'chuff, chuff, chuff' through the air and then count, 'One, two, three' as it comes into the station in the open mouth!
● Make your spoon into an aeroplane, flying around until it lands with a 'one, two, three' into the mouth!
● When your baby is older, you can enjoy this rhyme, knocking gently on your child's forehead for the first line, touching his nose for the second and popping in the spoonful of food for the third:

    Knock at the door,
    Turn the handle,
    Open wide,
    And *in* we go!
    (Traditional, adapted by Hannah Mortimer)

● Another helpful ruse you can try is to sit Teddy in a chair next to your baby and say, '*One* for Teddy, *one* for *(your child's name)*!' and so on.
● Try to keep mealtimes relaxed and enjoyable to avoid problems – children usually balance their food intake naturally, eating just what they need over a period of time. If you are worried about your child's feeding, talk with your health visitor.

Taking it further
● Keep portions small so as not to outface your child, and praise him when it is 'all gone'. You can always come back for 'more'!
● Remember to be prepared for mess at this early stage – it is all part of the learning process.

AGE RANGE
0–1 year

LEARNING OPPORTUNITIES

● To develop finger-feeding
● To enjoy mealtimes
● To link spoken numbers to quantity.

YOU WILL NEED

Soft toast and spreads; baby plate; knife for yourself.

Toast soldiers

Sharing the game

● This game is best for older babies who are learning to finger-feed and can handle rusks and toast fingers.

● Make some toast and spread it straight away with butter or spread, so that it stays soft.

● Add some of your baby's particular favourite topping, such as a little honey or fruit spread.

● Take off the crusts and cut the toast into fingers about the size and shape of baby rusks.

● Arrange these on a plate, side by side, and place it on your baby's high-chair table in front of her.

● As she eats each one, count it for her, saying, 'One gone!', then count the remaining toast 'soldiers' for her, saying, 'How many left? One… two...' and so on.

● Although she is much too young to say or understand numbers herself, you are teaching her that numbers are fun and are something

to do with 'how many' of an item there are.

● Your older child will enjoy counting with you. Arrange the soldiers in a line so that they are easier to count.

Taking it further

● Begin to introduce the word 'lots', saying, '*Lots* of toast!'.

● Use 'All gone!' when your child's plate is empty and offer, 'More?' if it is appropriate.

MEALTIMES

AGE RANGE
1–2 years

LEARNING OPPORTUNITIES
● To explore quantity
● To respond to 'lots'.

YOU WILL NEED
Your usual feeding equipment; suitable food that is made up of particles, such as baked beans, couscous, rice and so on; a spoon for each of you.

Lots and a little

Sharing the game

● In this game, you and your toddler enjoy sharing a plateful of food together.
● Place a suitable quantity of the same food on to a plate between you.
● Start your toddler off with a few spoonfuls while he is hungry – either by feeding him or encouraging him to use his own spoon, depending on the stage he is at.

● Then use your spoon to separate the quantity into two, saying, '*Lots* for *(your child's name)*, *a little* for Dad!' (if you are Dad).
● After a few more mouthfuls, divide the plateful again and say, 'Lots for Dad! A little for *(your child's name)*!'.
● When you have done this for a while, you can play a game helping yourselves on to two plates from one serving bowl, again pointing out who has 'lots' and who has 'a little'.
● You can also use these words as you serve out biscuits, crisps, pieces of fruit, sultanas and so on.

Taking it further

● Most young children become faddy eaters at some stage. You may be able to persuade your child to finish eating something by dividing the food on his plate into two and saying, 'Eat *this* and leave *this*'. That way, you have compromised and you may be able to avoid a battle of wills!

LEARNING OPPORTUNITIES
● To understand 'more' and 'less'
● To practise drinking skills.

YOU WILL NEED
A plastic pouring jug; two clear plastic cups or beakers; your toddler's favourite juice or drink; clean washing-up bowl.

More juice, please!

Sharing the game
● Part-fill the jug with some of the juice.
● Pour the juice as your toddler watches, making sure that you pour a little into one beaker and a lot into the other.
● Offer your toddler a choice, asking her whether she would like *a little* juice or *lots* of juice. Point to each as you say the words.
● Guide her hand if you need to in order to help her to drink all by herself. Use a lidded beaker with two handles if this is easier.
● Offer your toddler more juice and encourage her to watch as you pour it. Because you have chosen clear beakers, she will be able to watch how the quantities change as they fill up.

● Now fill the jug with water and take the beakers and jug outside for your toddler to enjoy a pouring and splashing game with the washing-up bowl.

Taking it further
● Encourage your toddler to ask for 'more' as soon as she can use a few words herself. If necessary, say the word first as a question for her to echo, for example, 'More?' to encourage her to say, 'More!'.
● Use the word for repeating an action, too. If she is enjoying a swing or a cuddle, offer, 'More?'. She will learn that 'more' means both more of a quantity and also more of something that is happening.

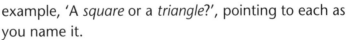

MEALTIMES

AGE RANGE
1–2 years

LEARNING OPPORTUNITIES
● To recognise shapes
● To link counting with quantity
● To enjoy mealtimes.

YOU WILL NEED
Soft sliced bread; spreads and favourite fillings; knife for yourself; pastry cutters or cup; dark plate.

Shapely sandwiches

Sharing the game
● Prepare some sandwiches for you both for a mealtime.
● Remove the crusts, then cut the sandwiches into different shapes, such as triangles, circles (using a pastry cutter or cutting around an upturned cup), squares and rectangles.
● Arrange these on a dark plate so that the shapes are easy to see.
● Count the number of sandwiches for your toddler, moving his finger as you count if he will allow you to. Count how many are left as they are eaten.
● Enjoy your meal together and name the shape for him as he chooses his next sandwich.
● Offer a named choice, asking your toddler, for example, 'A *square* or a *triangle*?', pointing to each as you name it.

● Your older child will love watching you and helping you to prepare the sandwiches.

Taking it further
● Play a game counting the round plates on the table for your toddler and counting the square windows. Here again, you are teaching him that numbers are interesting and fun long before he can manage to count for himself.
● Arrange your toddler's finger food in interesting shapes, patterns or 'faces' on his plate. This will make eating more interesting and engage his imagination.

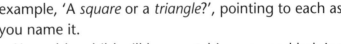

AGE RANGE
1–2 years

LEARNING OPPORTUNITIES
● To develop an awareness of counting
● To use a fork.

YOU WILL NEED
Favourite foods, such as chips, apple slices, seedless grapes, banana slices and mini savouries; two plates; serving dish.

One potato, two potato

Sharing the game
● In this game, you share food between the two of you.
● Place two plates in front of you both and point out which is your child's and which is yours.
● Bring out the serving dish and begin to serve the pieces of food, first serving one on to your toddler's plate and then serving one on to your own.
● As you share out the chips, chant this traditional rhyme:
    One potato, two potato, three potato, four!
    Five potato, six potato, seven potato, more!
● Substitute a new food word, depending on what you are sharing out, such as 'One banana, two banana, three banana, four' for pieces of banana!
● If you are waiting for food to arrive in a café or restaurant, you can also play a simple version of the following traditional and familiar game, using flat hands instead of fists: place your hand flat on the table and encourage your toddler to put hers on top, then place your second hand over hers and encourage her to add her second hand on top, then simply start again in a new position on the table.

Taking it further
● Your older child will enjoy sharing out the biscuits or snacks. Teach simple 'sharing into two' by chanting the rhyme as you share out. 'Sharing out' is the first stage of being able to divide numbers.

AGE RANGE
2–3 years

LEARNING OPPORTUNITIES
● To develop one-to-one correspondence when counting
● To match by colour.

YOU WILL NEED
A plastic toy tea set in primary colours (red, green, blue and yellow cup, saucer and plate); other objects to make an interesting pretend 'tea party'; teddy bear.

Teasets

Sharing the game
● Toy teasets are excellent for encouraging early colour-matching and one-to-one correspondence.
● You may have to do very little in this game – just watch your child play naturally and see how well he can match cup to saucer and colour to colour.
● Play alongside him as he makes you 'tea'. Make the game more interesting by blowing on your tea to make it cooler, or by asking for 'another biscuit'.
● Introduce a mischievous teddy bear who muddles all the colours up. Can your child put the right cups back on to the right saucers?
● Can your child find enough cups to go on all the saucers?

● Can he sort the cups, the saucers and the plates to put them away?
● Name the colours naturally as you play together. You do not need to cross-examine him with questions such as, 'What colour is this?' – he is more likely to name colours spontaneously as you play together.
● Count how many cups, saucers, plates you need for your tea party.

Taking it further
● Have a real tea party outside on a summer's day. Invite the teddy bears and cuddly toys and arrange the cups and saucers for them.
● Look for other games and toys that involve colour-matching, such as placing green shapes into green holes.

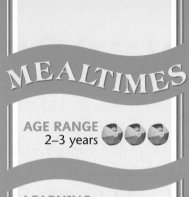

LEARNING OPPORTUNITIES
● To complete a simple mealtime shape board
● To match by picture, colour and shape
● To link counting to quantity.

YOU WILL NEED
A mealtime inset board; cardboard; scissors; old magazines; glue; felt-tipped pens for yourself.

Puzzle it out!

Sharing the game
● Start by playing with the mealtime inset board together. This is a board that has inset shapes of a knife, fork, spoon, plate and cup. Your child will enjoy removing the pieces for you to put back together again!
● As you play, talk about mealtimes and count the pieces that your child has removed or the spaces left to refill. If necessary, help her

by aligning the pieces next to their spaces. You can also put all the pieces back except one, encouraging her to place the last piece in position herself.
● Now make your own mealtime shape board for you and your child to enjoy together. Start with a sheet of cardboard about the size of a small tray. Draw on bold lines with a felt-tipped pen to outline where the plate, knife, spoon and so on should go. Then cut out shapes from cardboard to match, sticking on magazine pictures of plates of food or drawing on a knife, fork and so on.
● Encourage your child to watch or help as you play together.
● Help your child to match the shapes on to her board until it looks as if dinner is ready!

Taking it further
● Give your child support and encouragement to count out the items and help you to lay the table for two. You can make this easier by creating a second cardboard shape board and using both boards to match the plates, knives and so on, on to.

LEARNING
OPPORTUNITIES
● To begin to count
● To finish a meal
successfully.

YOU WILL NEED
Your usual food and
feeding equipment; three
identical spoons.

Three more mouthfuls

Sharing the game

● Save this game for the end of a meal when your child's appetite is beginning to flag and his interest is waning.

● When he has nearly finished, tell your child that he only needs to eat 'three more mouthfuls'.

● Chant this rhyme to him and enjoy the counting as you reach for three spoons:

Nearly time to leave the table –
Three more spoonfuls if you're able.
You'll be full as full as can be –
Three more mouthfuls: ONE, TWO, THREE!
Hannah Mortimer

● Count the spoonfuls as you fill them for your child and place them on the side of his plate, one after the other.

● Then repeat the rhyme and count the last line slowly and loudly as he pops each into his mouth. Clap and praise him at the end!

Taking it further

● Your older child will be able to count the three mouthfuls himself. Again, by seeking a compromise, you are staying in control, yet offering him choices and independence. This democratic way of managing mealtimes is a good recipe for co-operation!

● Offer small portions, so that your child is likely to finish his plateful, rather than full platefuls, which tend to force him to leave something.

Tasty faces

Sharing the game
● Use this game to enjoy a salad or fruit meal together.
● Cut up the foods, fruit and vegetables into interesting shapes.
● Place these on a large dish within reach of your child.
● Take your child to wash and dry her hands, encouraging her to be as independent as possible.
● Give her a plate and encourage her to make patterns and shapes with the pieces.
● Arrange your own shapes on to your plate to make a face or an interesting pattern. You might decide to have banana slices for eyes, a cucumber smile, a grape nose, curly crisps for the hair, apple slices for cheeks, and so on.

● Use your child's particular favourite foods to make your patterns together.
● Compare your patterns and talk about what they look like.
● Put them on one side until it is time to eat.
● Talk about each item of food as your child eats it, saying, for example, 'Was the nose good?', 'Enjoy your banana mouth!' and so on.
● As the pieces are gradually eaten, count them out loud and say, for example, 'Just three left' and so on.

Taking it further
● Some two-year-olds are much more likely to eat their meals if you can develop ideas and games like this one for keeping mealtimes fun and relaxing.
● Look for other opportunities to present food attractively and to provide smaller portions in order to encourage your child to empty her plate.

AGE RANGE
2–3 years

LEARNING OPPORTUNITIES
● To recognise and form simple numbers
● To enjoy snack time.

YOU WILL NEED
Flour; cornflour; butter or margarine; castor sugar; salt; cardboard; pen; scissors and small sharp knife for yourself; rolling-pin; board; baking tray; wire rack; oven; coated chocolate beans; jelly sweets; currants; hundreds and thousands; icing sugar; food colouring.

THINK FIRST!
Take care to keep your child away from heat and dangerous utensils when cooking together.

Number biscuits

Sharing the game
● Make some cardboard templates of numbers by drawing number shapes about 8cm high on to cardboard and then cutting these out.
● Wash your hands and enjoy mixing the biscuit dough together.
● Sift 350g plain flour and 175g cornflour into a bowl. Rub in 350g butter or margarine until the mixture resembles fine breadcrumbs. Stir in 175g castor sugar and a pinch of salt, and work the ingredients together to form a soft dough.
● Alternatively, place the ingredients into a food processor, well away from your child, and process until the dough is formed.
● Help your child to grease the baking tray with a little butter or margarine while you cool the dough for half an hour or so in the fridge.

● Roll the dough out on to a floured board until it is 0.5cm thick.
● Place the templates on to the dough and use your knife to cut around them.
● Lift the dough numbers on to the baking tray and bake at 300°F/150°C/Gas Mark 2 for 20–25 minutes. Cool on a wire rack.
● When the number biscuits are cool, ice and decorate them and enjoy naming them as you eat them!

Taking it further
● Make domino biscuits, using coloured chocolate beans or jelly sweets as the dots. Line them up before tucking in!

LEARNING OPPORTUNITIES
● To learn to share
● To count to five.

YOU WILL NEED
Simple snacks for sharing; your child's friends or teddy bears; a plate for each person.

Snack time

Sharing the game

● You can play this game either with a group of your child's friends or with teddy bears.

● Sit down in a circle and ask your child to share out the plates – can he put one plate in front of each person?

● Now introduce the snack, for example, a bowl of seedless grapes or a packet of biscuits.

● Explain to your child that you have a problem – you need to share the snack out, but how can you do this?

● Ask your child to help as you put first one item on to each plate, then two, then three and so on.

● Stop each round to count out how many each person has. Has everyone got the same number? If you are entertaining the bears, help your child to count how many snacks each bear has. Point to each snack as you count it together.

● Continue until you have shared the snack out fairly.

● Your older child will be able to share the snacks out himself if you stay close to encourage him.

Taking it further

● Start introducing simple fraction words, such as 'half'. As you cut a bun into two, say, '*Half* for you, *half* for me'.

● Work out together how many pieces to cut a small cake into, asking your child how many friends he can count around the table.

● Birthday cakes with candles provide wonderful opportunities for counting and sharing out.

CHAPTER 4

OUT AND ABOUT

Outings, walks and shopping trips are the perfect opportunities for children to find out about shapes, sizes and numbers in the world around them and to talk about simple patterns and designs. Many of the games in this chapter can be adapted for older or younger children and your child can take part in them in different ways, depending on the stage he is at. Try dipping into all the games for ideas, whatever age and stage he has reached.

SEEING SHAPES

The ability to see the difference between shapes and to respond differently to them (known as 'discrimination') develops very early on in human beings. It is a basic skill that all animals and humans need to have in order to identify sources of food, danger and comfort. In fact, studies on octopuses have shown that they are well able to spot a square or a triangle if their food is always hidden behind one! In the same way, your new baby will soon become able to identify you from your general shape and movement, your facial features, your smell and your voice. You will notice her move her body more as she sees you approach, or perhaps 'still' to the sound of your voice.

After a few months, she will begin to take an interest in objects and toys around her as well as faces. She will begin to make swiping movements with her arms and occasionally come into contact with these. From this point, she begins to make the links between seeing and reaching out towards something.

Your one-year-old will enjoy handling objects and toys, and will take a delight in posting things in, and emptying them out of, containers. By about 21 months, she will be posting round pegs into round holes and taking an interest in posting-box games. Around her second birthday, she will probably be able to match a circle, a square and a triangle to their correct places on a shape form board – typically, she will manage the circle first, then the square and later the triangle. When she is two, she will develop these skills and enjoy all kinds of simple shape boards and early jigsaws.

How you can help

● Use the same tone of voice and say your child's name as you approach her in her cot or cradle seat, so that she links your voice to your presence.

● Use a variety of brightly coloured baby toys of different shapes and textures for her to look at and explore with her hands and mouth.

● Introduce the words for different shapes early on, even if your child cannot yet understand these, for example, a *round* ball, a *square* box and so on.

● Provide her with brightly coloured three-dimensional shapes to handle and explore, such as cubes, boxes, balls and cylinders.

● Encourage her to play with shape-posting and shape-matching games as soon as she is interested.

BIG ONES, LITTLE ONES

It takes a while for your baby to develop the stereoscopic vision to be able to tell different sizes and distances apart – in other words, a small ball close-up will look the same to him as a large ball further away. As he begins to handle different sizes of objects, he will begin to develop a better understanding of this.

Your eighteen-month-old will probably be able to match a large circle to a large space on a shape board, and a small circle to a small space, using mostly a trial-and-error approach.

By the age of two, your child will probably enjoy placing different-sized nesting toys inside of each other, or stacking them to make a tower. He will point to the

'big' one or the 'little' one if you ask him to and he will begin to use these words spontaneously in his play.

How you can help

● Provide opportunities for your child to empty and fill containers so that he can develop an understanding of sizes and quantity.

● Look for chances to play pouring and filling games in the bath water or the sand-pit.

● Look for toys that involve grading different sizes, such as size shape boards, stacking rings, stacking beakers, size posting toys and so on.

● Use the words 'big' and 'small' or 'little' in your play together so that your child begins to link these words with the appearance of an object.

RECOGNISING PATTERNS

Young babies seem to be pre-programmed to take an interest in certain patterns of light and shade, and are predisposed to look at and study faces that come within their focus. After a few months, you will notice your baby staring intently at her own hands and fingers as if she has recognised for the first time that these waving objects belong to her! She will quickly learn to recognise the pattern that her fingers make and link these to the feelings of touch that she receives from them and the movements that she can make with them – this is very clever eye–hand co-ordination.

Even before three years old, your child will be able to spot and take an interest in numbers around her, and begin to realise that these are different from letters and words. She will be able to spot familiar numbers on road signs and on packaging and take a

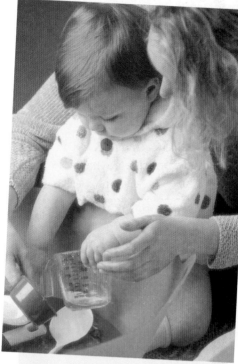

pride in 'reading' these to you, for example, 'Look! There's a 3!'.

How you can help

● Make written numbers a part of your child's life from early on – try number friezes for her wall, number mobiles over the changing mat, and toys and puzzles that feature numbers.

● Spot written numbers together as you handle shopping or go on journeys.

● Make a big occasion out of the birthday number so that she starts to recognise this number in different situations.

● Choose toys that involve pattern-making, for example, chunky beads or cotton reels to thread, coloured peg or mosaic boards, construction or interlocking toys to be pieced together in different arrangements, and so on.

● Look out for repeating patterns as you travel around together, such as the rails of a fence, the squares on a pavement and the count-down exit signs on a motorway.

LEARNING OPPORTUNITIES
● To anticipate what will happen next
● To enjoy a repeated sequence of movement
● To enjoy being sociable.

YOU WILL NEED
Your baby's pushchair or buggy.

Wheeee!

Sharing the game
● This game is fun for when your baby is between six and twelve months.
● Wait for a fine day and strap her into her pushchair or buggy. Talk to her all the time, even though she is too young to understand the words yet.
● Find a straight, clear path without people and obstacles around and slow the pushchair right down.

● Count slowly and steadily, 'One… two… three…' and then accelerate gently as you add, 'Wheeee!'.
● Slow right down again as you start your count and wait for the chuckles as you build up to the 'Wheeee!'.
● Repeat several times if your baby seems to be enjoying this.
● Then walk normally for a while and watch her. If she is making noises and kicking her arms and legs, then she is probably anticipating more fun!
● Try a few other sequences, pausing to say, 'More?' each time.

Taking it further
● Help your baby to notice the round shape of wheels by showing her the wheels on her toys and turning them together.
● Use the words, 'One… two… three…', as a lead in to other enjoyable activities.
● Repeat activities that your baby enjoys over and over, so that she begins to anticipate and to understand sequences of activity.

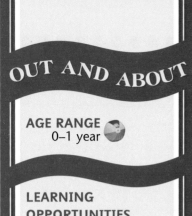

AGE RANGE
0–1 year

LEARNING OPPORTUNITIES
● To manipulate objects
● To develop an awareness of size.

YOU WILL NEED
Your baby's pushchair or removable car-seat, or a supermarket trolley if he is old enough to sit in one.

💡 **THINK FIRST!**
Watch out for your baby's safety – do not let him play with objects that could harm him or that he could choke on. Remove all plastic bags from his reach.

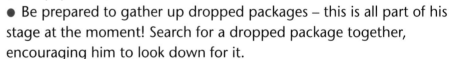

Big ones and little ones

Sharing the game
● Save this game to play with your baby when he is between nine and twelve months.
● Take him with you as you go shopping. Make it a short trip so that he does not become frustrated.
● As you reach for the packages, give your baby one that he can easily grasp and handle.
● Comment on the size or the shape as you hand it to him, saying, for example, 'Look! A *big* one!' (for a cereal package), 'Look! A *heavy* one!' (for a small tin), 'Look! A *long* one!' (for a paper roll) and so on.
● Be prepared to gather up dropped packages – this is all part of his stage at the moment! Search for a dropped package together, encouraging him to look down for it.
● When you get home, enjoy handling the packages as you unpack the shopping.
● Give your baby one low cupboard that is safe and that you do not mind him emptying and filling up again.

Taking it further
● Save empty packages in different shapes and sizes for your child to handle and play with.
● Try stacking empty boxes and making dens with cartons.
● Hide teddies loosely in paper bags to be found again!

LEARNING OPPORTUNITIES
● To explore containers
● To develop problem-solving.

YOU WILL NEED
Several clean paper bags; selection of your baby's toys.

Paper bags

Sharing the game
● Prepare for this game by hiding several of your baby's toys, one in each bag, and loosely scrunching the top of the bag together so that it is easy to open.
● Place the bags in the car, close to your baby's car-seat.
● When it is time to go for a car journey, strap her into her seat as usual and arrange the paper bags around her.
● Talk to her as you drive and as she explores, handles and mouths the bags.
● When she is a little older, she will enjoy shaking the bag to rattle the contents, and may even shake the toy out from the inside.
● She will then begin to 'make the connection' between looking inside the bag and finding a toy there.
● While she is doing all this exploring and discovering, she should be amused and occupied for part of your journey together.
● You can adapt this activity to play at any time and not just when you are in the car.

Taking it further
● Always keep one or two 'surprises' in the car to distract your baby on long journeys.
● If she is strapped in the back, make a set of pockets to hang over the back of the front seat for her to reach into and pull out toys from.
● When she is older, you will be able to challenge her to, 'Find the teddy' or, 'Find the ball' in the paper bags around her.

LEARNING OPPORTUNITIES
● To look and to listen
● To explore the outdoor world
● To recognise the numerals 1 and 2.

YOU WILL NEED
The rhymes 'Two little dicky birds', 'Two little jellyfish' and 'Two little butterflies' on page 127.

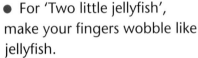

Two little dicky birds

Sharing the game
● These rhymes are fun to enjoy together when you are out walking or when you have a few moments to spare while waiting for the bus or at the supermarket check-out.
● Hold up two fingers, one from each of your hands as you chant 'Two little dicky birds' (Traditional). Then hold one up high and make it wave as you introduce 'Peter' and then the other for 'Paul'. Make your fingers disappear, one at a time, in line three and reappear again as you say the last line.

● For 'Two little jellyfish', make your fingers wobble like jellyfish.
● For 'Two little butterflies', make your fingers gently flutter around your child and then flutter them behind your back as they disappear 'home' at the end.
● If you are out walking, stop to watch the birds with him and then sing your 'dicky bird' rhyme together.
● Your younger baby will enjoy watching and listening to you and may giggle as the fingers reappear again. Your older child may begin to join in with the actions and some of the sounds.

Taking it further
● There are countless variations to this traditional rhyme. You could use your walks to spot new creatures to make up verses about: 'Two little ducklings swimming on the pond…', 'Two little fishes swimming in the stream…' and so on.
● Do not worry if your verses do not rhyme or scan. Use family names to make them more fun and to attract your baby's attention.

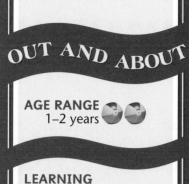
LEARNING OPPORTUNITIES
● To copy a sequence of actions
● To develop an awareness of written numbers.

YOU WILL NEED
A sandy beach or a path, yard or playground; seaside spade or piece of chalk; teddy bear.

Number trails

Sharing the game
● This is a lovely game to play on a trip to the seaside, or you can play it with chalk on a path or in a yard or playground.
● As you walk together across the sand, draw your toddler's attention to the footprints that you are both making. Spend some time making impressions in the sand together (or walk in wellington boots through puddles and watch your boot prints on the ground).
● Now use your spade to make a line in the sand. Make it curl and loop and place a teddy bear at the end. (If you are playing in a yard or playground, use chalk lines instead.)
● Hold your toddler's hand as you walk along the line, watching your feet as you go. Greet the teddy together at the end of your trail.
● Next, make a series of dashes (which are also straight '1's) instead of a solid line, so that you have to look around a bit to find the next '1'. Chant, 'One!' as you step on to each dash.
● For your older toddler, draw a series of '1's, leading into a series of '2's and finishing with a final '3' next to the teddy. Chant each number as you step on to it. Even though your child is too young to read the numbers, she will be starting to make links between the written patterns and your words.

Taking it further
● Make a number trail using the numbers 1, 2, 3, 4 and 5, and count the numbers as you step together from one to the next.
● Draw a simple 'Hopscotch' frame on the ground and say the numbers as you jump from square to square.

AGE RANGE
1–2 years

LEARNING OPPORTUNITIES
● To develop understanding of 'on top of' and 'underneath'
● To recognise and name the numbers 1 and 2.

YOU WILL NEED
A toddler climbing frame and slide in the garden or at the playground.

On top of the world!

Sharing the game
● Explore the climbing frame together and have fun helping your toddler to climb and slide for a while.
● When he climbs high, exclaim, 'You're *on top*!'. You can also introduce the words, '*(Your child's name)* is *high* now… *(Your child's name)* is down *low*!'.

● See if you can join in too by crawling beneath and saying, 'Look! Dad's *underneath* you!' (if you are Dad).
● Now play a game making a bridge with your legs and showing your toddler how to crawl underneath you, then saying, 'Look! Dad's *on top* of *(your child's name)*!'.
● If you feel able, you can also enjoy a 'rough and tumble', holding him above you and emphasising these different position words as you play together.
● Young children begin very early on to make links between the words that they hear and the actions that they are performing, so this will help your toddler to develop an understanding of position words later on.

Taking it further
● Play with cuddly toys and boxes together, again using the words 'on top of', 'beneath' and so on.
● Make a simple multi-storey car park out of two carton boxes, one on top of the other, and play with cars 'on top of' and 'underneath' the different levels.

LEARNING OPPORTUNITIES
● To handle different shapes and packages
● To be interested and involved.

YOU WILL NEED
A supermarket trolley with a safe child-seat; empty packages; scissors for yourself.

Shopping fun

Sharing the game
● Save some empty packages, such as your toddler's favourite cereal box, a clean, empty juice packet and so on.
● Collect three different items and cut out a distinctive panel from each to keep.
● Next time you visit the supermarket, sit your child comfortably in the trolley and give her one of the pieces of packaging to hold.
● Talk about what you are looking for, saying, for example, 'Where are the cereals?… Here? No!… Here? YES!'.
● Point out packages that are the same colour and design as the one that she is holding, and celebrate together when you find a full package that is the same as the panel.
● Take the item from the shelf and let your child handle it. She will be able to compare appearances and weights by handling and exploring all the different packages.

● Repeat the game for two or three other items.
● Keep the shopping trip short so that she does not become tired or frustrated.
● When you get home, give your toddler some full and empty packs to play with while you unpack the rest of the shopping.
● Introduce the words 'same', 'heavy', 'full' and 'empty' as you play together.

Taking it further
● Give your toddler a selection of cans or safe packages to play with on the floor. Can she find a pack that is just the same as one that you show her?
● Play a simple shopping game at home by arranging empty packs on a table and giving your toddler a shopping basket to fill.

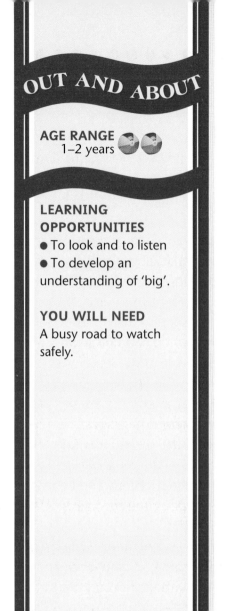

AGE RANGE
1–2 years

LEARNING OPPORTUNITIES
● To look and to listen
● To develop an understanding of 'big'.

YOU WILL NEED
A busy road to watch safely.

BIG lorry!

Sharing the game

● You can play this game when you are out together in a car or bus, or by looking out of a window on to a road.

● Draw your toddler's attention to the traffic going by. He will be just at the stage of wanting to 'label' everything that he sees and catches his interest, so call, 'Car!' together as one goes by.

● Point out any lorries going by as well, saying, ' Look! Lorry!' each time you see one.

● When your toddler seems able to recognise and name a lorry, begin to share your excitement together as soon as you see a really big lorry going by!

● Each time you see a big lorry, draw your toddler's attention to it and announce, 'BIG lorry!'.

● After a while, you will begin to hear him echo this two-word phrase, probably using your tone of voice as well.

● Now you can begin to introduce the word 'big' to other objects too, thus helping your toddler to 'generalise' the word to many different things. Generalisation is a crucial part of language and number learning.

Taking it further

● Play with big and small balls, and big and small toy cars and lorries. Use the words 'big' and 'little' naturally as you play together.

● Emphasise the word 'big' by using an expansive open arm gesture and saying, 'What a BIG one!'.

LEARNING OPPORTUNITIES
- To count to three
- To respond to 'more'.

YOU WILL NEED
A small shopping trolley or basket.

Helping hands

Sharing the game

- When you are out shopping, look for ways of involving your child and allowing her to 'help'. She has now reached the stage when she needs to feel more independent.
- Start by emphasising any safety rules that you have for when you are shopping, such as always holding hands or always staying close to Mum, Dad or Grandma.
- Then ask your child if she would help you today. Show her the shopping basket – some supermarkets have child versions of their trolleys, which are excellent for this game.
- As you approach each aisle, give your child a new challenge: 'Can you find me *one* tin of beans?', 'Can you find me *two* packs of juice?' and so on.

- Show her where the items are to be found and help her lift one, two or three into her basket, then carry them to your trolley.
- She should be able to help with most of the shopping in this way.
- Let her carry a few light items to the check-out herself in her own basket or trolley.
- Include one or two treats for when you get home to thank her for helping you.

Taking it further

- You can now enjoy simple shopping games at home with plastic 1p and 2p coins. Label the items with a '1' or a '2' and take it in turns to be shop assistant.
- Encourage your child to watch and listen as you count out money for your shopping. She will soon understand that shopping is about handing over a quantity of coins in order to buy something new.

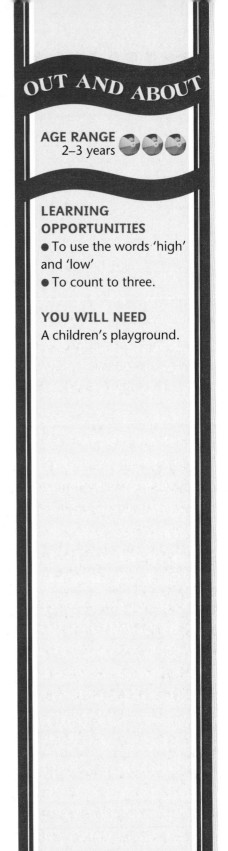

AGE RANGE
2–3 years

LEARNING OPPORTUNITIES
● To use the words 'high' and 'low'
● To count to three.

YOU WILL NEED
A children's playground.

Ready, steady, slide!

Sharing the game

● Find out where your nearest playgrounds are. The best will have safety flooring beneath the equipment and a fenced area to keep children in and animals out.

● Visiting playgrounds can be a cheap and entertaining way to plan your days or holidays, and provides endless amusement for your child.

● Stay close at all times to watch for his safety, to make it fun and to talk about what he is doing.

● Help him to carefully climb the slide and turn himself safely into a sitting position.

● Now encourage him to pause as you count slowly, 'One, two, three…', and then to slide down on your '… DOWN!'. Repeat for several turns.

● When he is climbing, count the steps of the slide, then point out how 'high' he is.

● As you push your child on the swings, chant out loud, 'High… low' as he swings.

● Climbing frames provide plenty of opportunities for using these position words naturally and as a way of sharing fun.

● After a while, you will find that your child understands and then begins to use these words himself.

Taking it further

● Sing 'The Grand Old Duke of York' (Traditional) as you swing your arms 'high and low' and 'march up and down the hill'.

● Count as you walk up steps and down steps.

 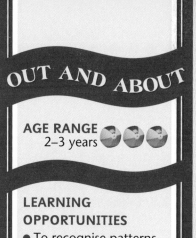
LEARNING OPPORTUNITIES
● To recognise patterns
● To count steps with help.

YOU WILL NEED
A zebra crossing to negotiate.

Zebra crossings

Sharing the game

● This is a chant to learn and say together as you cross the road on a zebra crossing:

Now we need to cross the road –
Cross it safely, holding hands.
First look out for the zebra crossing;
Stop at the kerb for the traffic passing.
First look left, and then look right –
Are there moving cars in sight?
Now it's safe to cross the road –
One, two, three, four, holding hands.
Hannah Mortimer

● Start by learning it together at home until you are familiar with the words.

● Then act out the sequence as you pretend to cross a road at home. Pretend to look out for the crossing, watch for the traffic coming and then walk safely across it, holding hands.

● Now, you are ready to take a walk together. Encourage your child to tell you the safe place to cross. Ask her to look out for the zebra crossing.

● Chant the rhyme as you go through the sequence of actions and congratulate your child for crossing safely and sensibly.

● Count the black and white stripes as you cross together.

Taking it further

● Talk about road safety as you are out walking together.

● Choose a few important rules and make sure you stick to them, such as always wearing seat belts in the car and always holding hands near to a busy road.

● Look out for any other patterns as you walk, such as iron railings beside a path, the windows on a skyscraper, the lines on the pavement and so on.

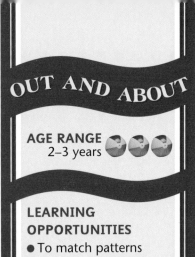
LEARNING OPPORTUNITIES
● To match patterns
● To count objects and trace over numbers.

YOU WILL NEED
Empty packages and cans; cardboard box; paper; pencil.

Lots of lists

Sharing the game
● Save some suitable empty packages and the wrappers of empty cans as you finish them.
● Keep these together in a cardboard box until it is time to go shopping again.
● Explain to your child that you would like him to help you to make a shopping list. You need to replace everything that was used last week.

● Bring out the packages and sort them into sets – put the baked-beans-can wrappers in a row, the empty juice cartons in another row, the empty biscuit packs in a third row, and so on.
● Help your child to count each row, moving his finger and counting with him if necessary.
● Write the number for him lightly in pencil on a piece of paper and help him to trace over it.
● Now write in the item to buy – for example, if your child was counting empty crisp packs, help him to trace over a '6', then write in 'packs of crisps'.
● In the shop, involve your child by helping him to count out the items into your trolley.

Taking it further
● Your older child will be able to copy some of the lettering to make a simple shopping list.
● You can also stick your packages on to a list and use it for you both to shop with. Talk about items that look the same and different as you decide what to buy together.

CHAPTER 5

BUSY TIMES

Art, craft and early mark-making help young children to recognise, name and write simple numbers and sets. Written numbers can be introduced to children long before they are ready to count them out or name them. If this is done in an enjoyable and relaxed way, children can then learn that numbers are fun to play with and non-threatening.

NUMBER-SPOTTING

In Chapter 4, we noted that the ability to see the difference between shapes and to respond differently to them (known as 'discrimination') develops very early on. If your child is to be able to 'recognise' number shapes and discriminate these from letters and other shapes, she will first need to develop her observation skills and her ability to perceive different shapes, rotations and lines. So all the games that you are playing to develop shape recognition will also be helping your child's ability to spot and 'read' written numbers later on. Your one-year-old will enjoy joining in a single clap for 'One!' and you can link this to one candle on the birthday cake, or a number 1 on an age badge, chanting, 'How many?…

One!'. By about two, she will be playing posting games and might also enjoy fitting numbers in to the shaped form boards.

How you can help
● Try to make numbers familiar and fun, using, for example, a number mobile, wall chart or poster that you can talk about even before your child is old enough to understand.
● Make use of natural opportunities to spot numbers, such as on birthday cards and house numbers. Point these out to your child and look out for the number that is the same as her age.
● Look out for toys that have numbers as part of them – there are many form boards, puzzles and early number toys available now that you can play with, long before your child can understand 'maths'.

NAMING NUMBERS
Before your child can make the link between written numbers (for example, '2') and 'how many' these represent (such as 'two cups'), he will have to develop an understanding of 'sets' (different quantities of objects). That is why some of the games that you will play in this chapter do not have any written numbers at the early stages, but are played to help your baby to make links in his thinking

between different quantities and sets. This is to emphasise that understanding numbers involves far more than recognising and reading numbers – your child has to grasp how to use numbers and how they relate to different amounts of things.

How you can help

● Provide opportunities for sorting and matching games using objects that are safe and easy to handle – coloured building blocks, toy animals, plastic ducks and so on.

● Make sure that early counting is part of your games by giving your child sets made up of lots of the same thing, for example, cotton reels, spoons, shoes and so on.

● When you count out the cups for tea, or the videos to go in the cupboard, for example, say the number and then point to the corresponding written number on a wall frieze, mobile or poster.

● Use number badges to show your child's age at birthdays.

WRITING IT DOWN

Children tend to start writing numbers at ages three to five, but it will take a while before they can form these correctly. Usually they write '1', '2' and '3' before they make an attempt at higher numbers. Before she reaches the stage of being able to copy or remember how to write a number, your child will need to learn how to control a crayon or felt-tipped pen, make straight lines and draw circular lines.

Before she can learn how to write numbers to represent a quantity of something, she will need to make links between what numbers *look like*, what they *feel* like to write and *how many* they represent. Again, by playing with your child from an early age, matching, posting, scribbling, holding and manipulating, you will be teaching her all the hand–eye co-ordination skills that she needs to learn to write numbers later on. By adding your own commentary to help her to count and point out what written numbers 'say', you will also be helping her to make the links between counting, writing and reading numbers.

How you can help

● Provide your child with early shape-matching toys and interesting objects to handle and explore so that she develops her ability to make links between what she sees and how her hands move.

● Look for writing and drawing implements that are good for small hands to hold, such as chubby crayons, egg-shaped chalks, finger crayons and so on. You can help your child to refine her skills by giving her finer pencils and felt-tipped pens later on as she controls her grasp better.

● Show your child how to make straight lines and circular scribbles and let her enjoy mark-making.

● Write numbers in yellow felt-tipped pen for her to copy over – keep these large at first, and guide her hand if she will let you.

● Look for opportunities for your child to make links between the number that she is writing and actual counting, for example, three ducks in the bath, or two plates on the table.

● Celebrate all success – your child will not write perfectly, but you need to show her how well she is doing!

BUSY TIMES

AGE RANGE
0–1 year

LEARNING OPPORTUNITIES
● To explore by feeling
● To empty and fill containers
● To play with sets.

YOU WILL NEED
A clean, metal waste-paper basket, or a biscuit tin; selection of objects that can be sucked and touched safely, such as a rattle, ball, plastic toy, metal spoon and so on.

Bin it!

Sharing the game

● Choose a container that will make an interesting noise when hard things are dropped into it, such as a metal waste-paper basket.

● This game is best for babies of six months or over. Wait until the stage when your baby is ready to hold out and then release a small toy.

● Give him a small toy to hold and encourage him as he explores it with his hands and mouth.

● Hold out your hand to him and say 'Thank you', as he passes the toy to you, and then drop it into the container, saying, 'All gone!'.

● Offer the container to your baby so that he can look for the toy and perhaps reach in to retrieve it.

● After a few turns, encourage him to drop the toy in himself.

● Repeat with several objects – your baby will be making links in the way the objects feel and the noise that they make as they fall.

● Play for several minutes, retrieving and dropping the toys until your baby's interest begins to wane.

● As you hand each object to your baby, say, 'Here's *one*!'. As he drops it in, say, 'All gone!'.

Taking it further

● Once your baby is familiar with the ritual of dropping in and retrieving a toy from a container, give him a whole set of the same kind of object to play with. For example, give him empty cotton reels to drop into an aluminium bowl, or plastic animals to drop into an empty ice-cream tub.

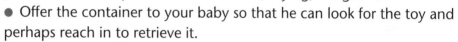

AGE RANGE
0–1 year

LEARNING OPPORTUNITIES
● To link cause with effect
● To develop awareness of numbers
● To enjoy being sociable.

YOU WILL NEED
Three pieces of card; felt-tipped pen for yourself; three tea towels; six cuddly toys.

Lots of cuddles

Sharing the game
● In this simple game, you can introduce written numbers long before your child is ready to recognise them or name them, to help her to make links between written numbers and counting.
● Play it when your baby has reached the stage of looking underneath something to find what is hidden beneath.
● Draw a clear '1', '2' and '3' on to the pieces of card, one number on each card.
● Wait until your baby is taking a nap and then arrange the soft toys around the bedroom or living-room floor in the following sets: one toy next to the number '1', two toys next to the number '2' and three toys next to the number '3'.
● Cover each set of toys with a tea towel, leaving only the number card showing.
● When your baby has woken up and is ready to play, take her into the room where you placed the toys. Make a game of finding the tea towel next to the number '1' and wondering what you can find underneath it. Point to the '1' and say, 'Here's *one*!' as you lift off the first cloth.
● Give the toy a cuddle together.
● Repeat for the remaining sets, giving two cuddles and then three cuddles as you discover the other two sets of toys together.

Taking it further
● Soon your baby will crawl towards the cloths herself to see what is underneath them.
● When she gets older, you will be able to help her to arrange the toys herself in sets of one, two and three, matching the sets to the written cards.

BUSY TIMES

AGE RANGE
0–1 year

LEARNING OPPORTUNITIES
● To learn to vocalise
● To link cause and effect
● To repeat sounds.

YOU WILL NEED
Your baby's usual baby seat or rocking cradle.

Echo time

Sharing the game

● This is a lovely game for young babies of two months and above who are just beginning to make different sounds with their voices.

● Sit your baby in his seat or cradle so that he is slightly supported and looking at you.

● Attract his attention with a gentle touch, a jiggle of the toe or a rock of the cradle.

● Talk softly as you encourage him to look at your face.

● Now make single sounds

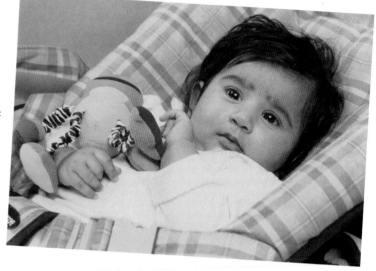

to him, which are similar to those he can make himself. Try, 'Aaa!' or, 'Ba!' to begin with.

● Leave a pause after each sound to allow your baby to repeat it if he wants to.

● If he does, then say the sound again until you are playing a 'My turn, your turn' game together.

● If he makes a different sound, then repeat that too.

● Make your sounds long, such as, 'Aaaaaaaaa!', and short, such as, 'Gu!', and see if you can encourage your baby to echo the length of the sound too.

Taking it further

● Your older baby will be able to echo you when you make one sound or two sounds, such as, 'Bu!' or, 'Bu bu!'. Try making a long string of sounds, for example, 'Bu bu bu bu bu!', and see if he makes a long string, too.

● You can also play the echo game by holding a rattle each and making sounds together.

AGE RANGE
0–1 year

LEARNING OPPORTUNITIES
● To develop an awareness of round shapes
● To link cause with effect
● To link hand sign with action.

YOU WILL NEED
Somewhere to roll down a hill; armchair; flat sheet of smooth wood or plastic (optional), such as a tray; selection of toys and balls.

Roly poly

Sharing the game
● This game is best for babies who are just learning to roll over and to sit up.
● Wait for a sunny day and find a suitable gently inclined grassy bank to play and roll on.
● Encourage your baby to gently roll down, supporting her as she turns and keeping this fun.
● When you ask her, 'More?', roll your

hands around each other to make a rolling sign. Watch her face and movements to see whether she wants to roll again.
● When you get home, play a rolling game together on the carpet.
● Place a toy just out of your baby's reach and encourage her to roll towards it. Support her head as she turns until she is good at this.
● Now lift her securely into an armchair and stay close to support her. Make a simple incline out of your piece of wood or plastic and prop it up against the front of the armchair.
● Hand your baby a ball and show her how to roll it down the incline. Make the 'roll' hand sign each time and cheer as the ball rolls away from her.
● Try rolling other toys too, less successfully.
● Only make your roll sign for round objects that roll successfully.

Taking it further
● You can also enjoy rolling and climbing at a baby-and-toddler soft-play centre.
● Sing 'Wind the Bobbin Up' (Traditional) together, making the roll sign with your hands.

LEARNING OPPORTUNITIES
● To explore number shapes
● To stick and paste.

YOU WILL NEED
Scissors and felt-tipped pen for yourself; selection of rough and smooth paper and card, including corrugated card and sandpaper if possible; pot of glue; glue brushes or spreaders; sheets of paper; plastic cloth.

Number shapes

Sharing the game

● Play this game when your toddler is just beginning to enjoy dabbing and making marks with a paintbrush or crayon.

● It is a good idea to have a large cardboard box or carrier bag in which to save old packaging and recyclable materials that are suitable and safe to use for craft.

● Have fun together choosing bits of paper and card that are interesting to feel and touch.

● Use your pen to mark two-dimensional number shapes (from 1 to 5) on to the pieces of card and paper, about 10cm high.

● Cut these out yourself or involve an older child to help.

● Allow your toddler to touch and handle the number shapes, saying the number to him as he explores each one.

● Now set up a gluing area, spreading a plastic cloth over a table and showing your child how to make dabs of glue on to the underside of each number shape. At this stage, he will enjoy handling and rubbing the paste, so be prepared for a mess – this is all part of the learning!

● Enjoy sticking the number shapes on to large sheets of paper to make number collages.

● Point to the numbers that your toddler has helped to stick on the paper and name them for him.

Taking it further

● Suspend number shapes from a string above the changing mat.

● Add sparkles and shiny stickers and make them into mobiles that twist and turn in the light.

LEARNING OPPORTUNITIES
● To match shapes
● To link written numbers with small sets.

YOU WILL NEED
A shape posting box and plenty of shapes to post, such as the Wooden Shape Sorter (Early Learning Centre); three sheets of coloured card; coloured felt-tipped pens for yourself.

Posting fun

Sharing the game
● Prepare for this game by writing a clear '1', '2' and '3', one on to each sheet of card. Underneath the numeral, draw one, two or three coloured circles, each large enough to place one of the posting shapes on top of it.
● Show your child the posting box and have fun posting in the shapes and then emptying out the container again.
● If your toddler will allow you to, gently guide her hands to fit the pieces in, but keep this fun.
● Start with shapes that are easy to post (such as discs and balls), then move on to more complex shapes (such as stars and crosses).
● Once your toddler is familiar with the toy, play a special number game. Give her one shape to post. Say, 'One!' as she pops it in the

box. Then empty it out and place it on the coloured circle on the '1' card. Say, 'One!' again as you point to the written number.
● Repeat this for two shapes and then three, so that each card is matched to one, two or three shapes.
● This is another example of a game where you are introducing written and spoken numbers in an enjoyable way even before your child is ready to count or read numbers. You are teaching her that numbers are familiar, easy and fun!

Taking it further
● Your older child will be able to match shapes to their spaces on the cards, count them out loud as they go on and then 'read' the number on the card.

AGE RANGE
1–2 years

LEARNING OPPORTUNITIES
● To develop an understanding of 'in' and 'down'
● To develop an understanding of 'next'
● To recognise numbers.

YOU WILL NEED
A cardboard tube, such as an empty foil roll; selection of bricks or other toys to send down the tube; large sheet of cardboard (about A2 size); felt-tipped pen; ruler; empty drawer.

Rolling down the tube

Sharing the game
● This is a simple way of introducing number shapes before your child is ready to recognise and name them, and it will help him to link numbers with enjoyment.
● Take a large sheet of cardboard – a side from a cardboard box would be fine – and use your ruler to divide it into nine squares – three across and three down.
● Write a number clearly, one on to each square, from '1' to '9'.
● Lift out an empty drawer that is just big enough to hold your cardboard sheet and place it on the floor.
● Tilt the tube up against the side of the drawer so that it ends on one edge of the cardboard – you are aiming for something that resembles a fairground 'Roll-a-penny' stall!

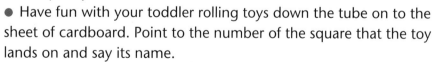
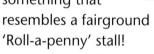

● Have fun with your toddler rolling toys down the tube on to the sheet of cardboard. Point to the number of the square that the toy lands on and say its name.
● Use the words 'in', 'down' and 'next' as you play together.

Taking it further
● Your older child of two to five will begin to recognise the numbers.
● Look for toys that roll easily and those that do not.

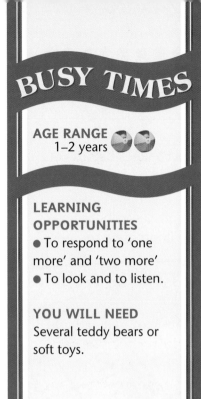
Hunt the bears

Sharing the game

● Hide up to five teddy bears or soft toys around the room, placing some behind beds or armchairs, some under covers and some behind cushions.

● Encourage your toddler to find the soft toys, and celebrate each discovery with '*There's* one!'.

● When you get to the last two, introduce the words, '*Two* more!' and, '*One* more!'.

● If your toddler begins to lose interest, hold her hand as you look for the toy together and ask, '*Where's* Floppy?… Is she here? No! Is she here? Yes!'.

● Now encourage your toddler to hide one or two of the toys for you to find. Keep the number small so that she begins to remember how many have been hidden altogether.

● At first, your toddler will not be able to resist showing you straight away! This is all part of the learning and you will still have to pretend to look hard!

● When you have found the first hidden toy, ask your toddler, 'Is there one more?'.

Taking it further

● Your older child will be able to find all the bears even if she does not know how many have been hidden, simply by listening to you saying, 'One more'.

LEARNING OPPORTUNITIES
● To discriminate between 'one', 'two' and 'three'
● To copy a sound
● To link sets to numbers.

YOU WILL NEED
A drum or plastic tub; three cards; paper; washable felt-tipped pens.

Drum calls

Sharing the game

● Sit down together at a table and get out the pens and paper.
● Enjoy scribbling and 'drawing' together for a while, then suggest that you play a game.
● Reach for the three cards and write a clear '1' on the first one. Show it to your child and ask him to repeat after you, 'One'.
● Now tell him that you would like to draw one thing on the other side of the card. Decide together what this will be (for example, a duck) and draw it on for him.
● Take the second card and write a clear '2' on one side. Decide together what you will draw on the other side, such as two cars.
● The third card will have '3' on one side and, for example, three teddy bears on the reverse. Now you are ready to play the drum game together.
● Take the first card and look at the number '1'. Say it out loud and then count one drum beat as you beat the drum with your hand. Turn the card over and count the object as your child makes one drum beat in reply.
● Repeat for the other two cards, helping your child to count out the objects as he makes each drum beat.
● Now try mixing the cards up – can your child still recognise the numbers with your help?

Taking it further

● Making cards with the numbers one side and sets of objects on the other is a useful way of teaching young children to read numbers. If they cannot recognise the number on one side, they can turn the card over and count the set with your help.

BUSY TIMES

AGE RANGE
2–3 years

LEARNING OPPORTUNITIES
● To explore shapes
● To practise early mark-making
● To develop early drawing skills.

YOU WILL NEED
Coloured paper; scissors for yourself; selection of chalks, crayons and washable felt-tipped pens; plastic tub; paper tray.

Up and down scribbles

Sharing the game
● Collect together all kinds of crayons, pens and chalks that are easy for little hands to hold, then place them in a plastic tub.
● Cut your coloured paper into many different shapes of all sizes, such as circles, squares, rectangles, triangles and stars. Place these in the paper tray.
● Set up an 'office' at the kitchen table and sit down to enjoy drawing together, talking about the shapes that you are using each time you select one to draw and make marks on.
● After a while, see if your child can copy you when you make a downward stroke on a shape. Say, 'Down' or, 'One!' as you make the mark.

● Practise making lots of strokes together.
● Now see if your child can copy you in making a 'round-and-round' scribble.
● Practise making lots of round scribbles together.
● Most written numbers are made up of straight lines and round shapes, so you are helping your child to get ready for number-writing later on.

Taking it further
● Look for different ways of making marks with your child, for example, by breathing on a mirror to mist it up and using your fingers to draw various shapes.
● As your child grows older, gently place the pen correctly into her fingers so that she learns how to hold it properly ('tripod' grip).

**LEARNING
OPPORTUNITIES**
● To explore textures
● To recognise numerals.

YOU WILL NEED
Snippets of different
materials and fabrics;
needle and embroidery
thread for yourself; old
cot cover; favourite
teddy or
soft toy.

Patchwork numbers

Sharing the game
● Make a simple 'number bed cover' by cutting numbers out of material and sewing them with embroidery thread on to an old cot cover or bed duvet cover. You might decide to use numbers 1 to 10, for example.
● Choose contrasting colours so that the numbers stand out clearly.
● You can work on this when your child is playing around you. Talk about which number you are sewing on now and build up his interest in what you are doing.
● When you have finished sewing, spread the cover out on the floor to admire your work. Help your child to point to each number as you say what it is.

● Then suggest that you show Teddy or another favourite soft toy all the numbers. Ask your child to 'jump' Teddy from number to number as you count one to ten for him. Help your child where necessary, in order to make sure that Teddy is being successful!
● Use the cover on your child's bed and enjoy playing the game again at bedtime.
● If you prefer, you can make a wall hanging or a table-cloth.

Taking it further
● Encourage your child to feel the shapes as well as to name them.
● You can also create a number place mat for your child to enjoy at meal times by making a colourful number card together, with felt-tipped pens or crayons, and have it laminated.

AGE RANGE
2–3 years

LEARNING OPPORTUNITIES
● To identify numbers 1 and 2
● To develop one-to-one correspondence.

YOU WILL NEED
Three pairs of coloured children's gloves; six cards; felt-tipped pens.

Hand in glove

Sharing the game

● Prepare for this activity by drawing a pair of gloves on the back of one of the cards, making it look identical in size and colour to one pair of the actual gloves.

● On a second card, draw just one of these gloves.

● Now repeat for the second pair of gloves, drawing one glove on one card and two on another.

● Finally, draw the third pair of gloves, again one on one card and two on another.

● Write a clear '1' or '2' on the front of each card, depending on whether that card shows one or two gloves on its reverse.

● You can make this game simple or hard, depending on the stage that your child has reached.

● Start by encouraging her to match one or two gloves to the pictures of one or two gloves. Do one card at a time and remember to cheer her success.

● Then show her the number side and ask her to give you that number of gloves. Turn the card over and try one-to-one matching to find out whether she was right.

● Finally, hold up the cards with the numbers showing and see whether your child can read the number '1' or '2' to you.

Taking it further

● You can use number cards with coloured stickers on the back to match to bricks or big buttons, too – that way you can build up towards higher numbers.

LEARNING OPPORTUNITIES
● To develop curiosity
● To name numbers
● To count to three.

YOU WILL NEED
Three little cardboard boxes, for example, small chocolate boxes; sticky labels; felt-tipped pens; six small toys or objects of interest, such as necklaces or other 'treasure'.

THINK FIRST!
Select toys that are small enough to fit into the boxes, but large enough not to be swallowed.

Secret treasures

Sharing the game
● Prepare for this game by hiding one object in one box, two in another and three in a third.
● Write '1', '2' or '3' on to three sticky labels and stick each to the corresponding box.
● Place the boxes around the room in different places.
● Challenge your child to hunt around the room for each box.
● When he finds one, ask him to guess how many things he will find inside the box.
● Open the box together and count out the objects.
● Talk about what you have found, then ask your child to hunt around to see whether he can find the other two boxes.
● Each time he finds one, encourage him to read the number to guess how many things are inside.

Taking it further
● Challenge your child to place one, two or three things inside the right boxes and hide them for you to find as well.
● Build up to higher numbers, for example, up to five.

AGE RANGE
2–3 years

LEARNING OPPORTUNITIES
● To match one to three objects to numbers
● To copy numbers
● To develop confidence with numbers.

YOU WILL NEED
An unused notebook; selection of different stickers; felt-tipped pens and scissors for yourself.

My number book

Sharing the game
● You can work together to make this book in order to build up your child's interest.
● On the first page, write the title 'My number book' and add your child's name.
● On the second page, write the number '1' on the top half of the page and encourage your child to stick one sticker beneath it, in the bottom half of the page.
● On the third page, write '2' at the top and ask her to stick on two stickers beneath.
● Continue until you have pages going up to '10', with ten stickers, or even higher if you wish.
● Each time your child adds the stickers, count them with her, stopping when you reach the number that you have written.

● Use your scissors to split the pages from page 2 onwards across the centre, so that the numbers are on the top part and the stickers are on the bottom part.
● Enjoy looking through this split-page book together, helping your child to match each written number with the right number of stickers underneath.

Taking it further
● Open one of the top pages to a number and then challenge your older child to find the right 'set' to go with it, for example, to find the six dinosaur stickers that go with the number '6'.

The games in this chapter will show you how to use movement, rhythm and physical play to encourage your child to follow directions, understand size and space, anticipate and copy action sequences, and respond to simple position and time words such as, 'up', 'down', 'before' and 'after'. These are all important aspects of mathematical development and you will be helping your child's progress by sharing movement and activity games that are fun and encourage self-confidence.

LIVELY TIMES

POSITION AND DIRECTION

Your baby's first experiences of position words, such as 'up' and 'down', will occur naturally as you lift her up and place her down throughout the day. From an early age, she will begin to anticipate what is going to happen when you greet her in the morning, wriggling into position or, later, raising her arms as you reach down to lift her.

One of her first words is quite likely to be 'up' or 'down' as you lift her or play repetitive games, since she knows that these words go hand in hand with a definite action or an intention.

When she is about one, she will delight in emptying and filling containers and will build up her understanding of 'in' and 'out' before she even has the language to understand what the words mean. At first, she will think that toys that fall out of her sight will be gone for ever, but once she understands the conservation of quantity – in other words that things continue to exist even when she cannot see them – she will begin to look underneath, in and behind objects to try to find them. The understanding of direction words such as, 'come', 'go',

'forwards' and 'backwards', tends to come a little later, when she has learned how to move around and how to change direction as she walks or trots, and also when she begins to understand abstract words, that is when she is about two years old.

How you can help

● Even when your baby is tiny, say 'up' and 'down' as you lift her and lay her down again.

● Provide plenty of toys and play things for your baby to put in containers and empty out again. Talk to her as she plays, emphasising the position words, for example, '*In* they go! *Out* they come!'.

● When your child is learning to walk, play a game with her and another adult, sending her first to the other adult, then the other adult sending her to you, as

you say, '*Away* you go! *Back* you come!'.
● Provide plenty of small-world play, such as a toy Noah's Ark, farmyard, garage, train track or dolls' house, and talk her through the position words, saying, for example, 'Look! Thomas is *in* the shed!'.
● Start asking 'where?' questions when she is older to encourage her to use position words in her talking.

UNDERSTANDING SIZE AND SPACE
Understanding of size and space develops naturally as your baby becomes more experienced in the objects around him. Cot covers and clothing all have interesting feels and textures, and he will soon learn that he can pull and tug these around to cover or uncover different parts of himself.

At first, he will not realise that a small car seen from close up is a different size from a large car seen from across a street. It is only by playing and interacting with

different-sized objects and experimenting with moving around himself that he will make links between distances, depths and sizes. This is when he will develop 'stereoscopic vision', allowing his two eyes to work together and linking this to his knowledge of how big things are in order to judge how far away they are.

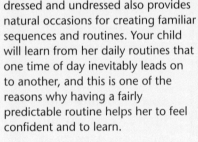

How you can help
● Provide plenty of practical and natural opportunities for your child to handle and touch objects and toys of different sizes, textures and shapes.
● Begin to provide him with simple containers and boxes for emptying and filling when he is a few months old.
● Make the most of sand and water play so that he can enjoy filling, pouring and sinking things, burying them, finding them again and so on.
● Provide a variety of shaped paper for drawing and scribbling on.
● Make sure that your child becomes familiar with shape- and size-matching puzzles and inset boards.

SEQUENCES OF ACTIONS
The first sequence that your baby will learn about is that one thing generally leads to another. This is also called 'linking cause with effect', and several of the earlier activities in this chapter will help your child to make these connections. Counting and numbers all follow given sequences and can develop out of her early attempts to carry out a simple sequence of actions. Some of the games will help you to build up

these little sequences of play. Getting dressed and undressed also provides natural occasions for creating familiar sequences and routines. Your child will learn from her daily routines that one time of day inevitably leads on to another, and this is one of the reasons why having a fairly predictable routine helps her to feel confident and to learn.

How you can help
● Build up familiar routines and rituals throughout the day for your child, such as giving a certain pattern to each day, a bedtime routine for settling her at night and so on.
● Make a visual timetable for your older child so that she can see from a sequence of photographs what is going to happen first each day and then what will happen next, for example, eating breakfast, going to nursery and so on.
● Introduce counting from an early age so that she begins to hear a familiar sequence of numbers, such as 'one, two, three'.
● Enjoy together action rhymes and games that will make repeating sequences of actions fun.

LEARNING OPPORTUNITIES
● To link cause with effect
● To experiment with sounds
● To respond to, 'more?'.

YOU WILL NEED
A pair of mittens; small rattle, large jingle bell or jingly teething ring; needle and strong thread for yourself.

💡 **THINK FIRST!**
Make sure that your baby cannot swallow small parts, and check regularly that your stitch work is secure.

Jingly fingers

Sharing the game
● Choose a pair of your baby's mittens that he cannot easily remove.
● Sew the rattle, bell or teething ring very securely on to the back of one of the mittens. Remove all loose threads.
● Wait until your baby is alert and interested, then put on his mittens.
● Gently shake the hand with the jingle on to make a sound.
● Leave his hand for a moment to see whether he moves it himself.
● If not, say, 'More?' and gently shake it again, drawing his attention to the sound.
● Enjoy making and repeating the jingly sound together. As he gets older, he will begin to move his hands purposefully in order to make and repeat the sound.
● Stay beside your baby to make this game sociable and to check that he does not chew the bell off.

Taking it further
● Attach jingles to booties and enjoy a musical kicking session.
● Turn an old pair of gloves into jingle gloves for your older child by sewing bells on to each fingertip.

AGE RANGE
0–1 year

LEARNING OPPORTUNITIES
● To explore through feeling
● To develop confidence
● To understand 'in' and 'out'.

YOU WILL NEED
A large cardboard box; light rug or cover; your usual soft furnishing; large scissors for yourself.

Small spaces

Sharing the game
● This game is best for when your baby is old enough to enjoy 'Peep-bo' games (see the game 'Peep-bo!' on page 26).
● Make your soft chairs into a den by placing them together and spreading the light rug or cover across the top, leaving one side open.
● Sit in your 'den' with your baby, enjoying the feel of the small space around you.
● Now prop your baby where she can watch you from outside as you creep inside the den and then pop your head out of the door or through the roof. Share the chuckling together!
● If your baby is already crawling, enjoy creeping in and out of view of each other.
● Now try a new experience: make a simple den out of a large cardboard box with the sides cut away.
● Place it on a smooth floor, such as a kitchen or bathroom floor.
● Again, enjoy your hiding and seeking, and spend time inside and outside the den together.
● Begin to use the words 'in' and 'out' as you play together.

Taking it further
● This is a lovely, simple game for your baby to play with older brothers and sisters.
● Make dens for the teddies and soft toys, and hide them inside for your baby to crawl and find.

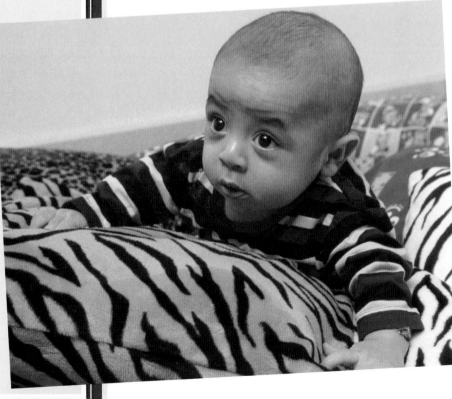

LIVELY TIMES

AGE RANGE
0–1 year

LEARNING OPPORTUNITIES
● To anticipate numbers
● To enjoy movement.

YOU WILL NEED
Just you and your child.

One, two, three, SWING!

Sharing the game

● If you are carrying your baby, chant, 'One, two, three, SWING!' as you swing him high. Start the words slowly and build up the climax.
● If your baby is starting to take weight on his feet, hold him by the waist and then swing him high, looking into his face as you do.
● Older children love to be swung between two adults holding their hands. Take care, however, to support tender joints and to keep this gentle if you swing your child in this way.

● Make a point of gaining your baby's attention first and emphasising the numbers as you say them.
● Pause just for a second or two before you give the swing and watch his eyes to see whether he is expecting it.
● Watch out for the point when your baby is beginning to anticipate what will happen next – he is now making connections and starting to understand simple sequences.
● Ask your baby, 'More?' before repeating the game.

● Soon, you will find that you can use, 'One, two, three…' to distract him from fretting when he is bored because he knows that something fun is about to happen.

Taking it further

● Use the 'One, two, three…' introduction when you are about to do something fun together, such as sharing a tickle, a cuddle or a gentle rough-and-tumble.
● Make mealtimes more interesting by using the 'One, two, three…' to introduce the next mouthful of your baby's favourite food.

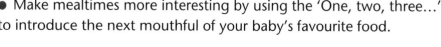

LEARNING OPPORTUNITIES
● To develop understanding
● To link words and actions.

YOU WILL NEED
Your baby's usual baby seat or rocking cradle, or cushions to prop her up.

So high!

Sharing the game
● Sit your baby in her seat, or lean her slightly up on cushions.
● Kneel opposite her and hold both her hands.
● Engage her attention by talking and smiling to her.
● Now gently raise and lower her two hands as you chant this rhyme:
SO high!
Fingers fly!
SO low!
Down they go!
Hannah Mortimer
● Raise your voice high for the first two lines as you hold your baby's hands high.

● Lower your voice for the last two lines as her hands are lowered down.
● Repeat this several times, trying to hold her eye contact all the time and keeping the game relaxed and enjoyable.
● In time, your baby might begin to raise her arms up high without your help when you say, 'SO high!'.
● If she does, give her a really big clap and praise her enthusiastically.
● This proves that you can enjoy action rhymes and action sequences together even before she is old enough to join in independently.

Taking it further
● Think of other simple action rhymes that you can perform with your baby, such as 'Round and Round the Garden' (Traditional).

LIVELY TIMES

AGE RANGE
1–2 years

LEARNING OPPORTUNITIES
● To develop balance
● To develop an awareness of simple position words.

YOU WILL NEED
A clothes line or rope; strong string; selection of lightweight soft and plastic toys.

THINK FIRST
Bend your knees and keep your back straight when lifting.

Reach and stretch

Sharing the game

● Stretch the clothes line or rope just a little higher than your child if you are outdoors.

● If you are indoors, find somewhere safe to secure a strong piece of string across a room, such as from a window catch to a coat peg.

● Prepare for this game by attaching three or four favourite toys to the line, loosely attached by string so that a pull will dislodge them.

● Show your toddler the toys and share the fun as he practises tottering towards them and reaching high to catch them.

● Give each toy a cuddle or a play as you detach it from the string.

● If necessary, support your toddler at the waist as he balances to reach high.

● If your child is older, you can encourage a jump too as he reaches even higher.

● Introduce the words 'high' and 'up' as you play together.

● Later, hang the toys higher up. Encourage your toddler to say, 'Up!' to you as you lift him towards them.

Taking it further

● Be aware that your toddler will now wish to climb everywhere in order to reach for things – look for opportunities where he can do this safely with you.

● If he is in danger, try saying, 'Come *down*!' rather than, 'Stop climbing!' – this gives him more information.

LIVELY TIMES

AGE RANGE
1–2 years

LEARNING OPPORTUNITIES
● To develop early counting
● To roll with aim.

YOU WILL NEED
Six cardboard cylinders, such as empty stacking-crisps boxes; large, soft sponge ball.

Knock them down!

Sharing the game
● Find a floor surface that is fairly smooth and even, and where there are no obstacles.
● Arrange the cylinders like skittles, one in front, two behind and three at the back, in a fairly tight cluster.
● If necessary, place something slightly heavy in the bottom of each 'skittle' to make it stand firmly, yet still allowing it to tumble.
● Sit down a few feet away, with your baby between your outstretched legs.
● Use your hands over hers to show her how to successfully push the ball away from her towards the skittles.

● Count, 'One, two, three…' before you push.
● Cheer merrily as you knock some of the skittles over.
● When your child is older, she will manage this herself, with your help, as you take turns to set up the skittles and roll the ball.
● Count how many skittles you have knocked down each time, drawing your child's attention to the number and encouraging her to repeat it after you.

Taking it further
● Roll a ball between you and your toddler, starting with a large ball and working down to a small one.
● Offer your toddler a basket for her to aim at when she is throwing a sponge ball. Say, 'One, two, three…' each time she throws.

Big steps, little steps

Sharing the game
● Put your boots on together and go outside.
● Make big puddles with the bucket of water by pouring splashes on to the ground. Alternatively, you can wait until it has just stopped raining.

● Enjoy a splash together in the puddles, stamping your boots.
● Show your toddler how he can make boot prints by stamping his wet boots on a dry patch of ground.
● Now enjoy making big steps and little steps as you make boot-print patterns on the ground.
● Say, '*Big* step' or, '*Little* step' when you make each stamp with your foot.
● When he is a little older, your child will copy your words and actions, but even now he will be making links between the patterns that he is creating and the words that you are saying to him.

Taking it further
● Use 'big' and 'little' frequently when you are handling everyday objects, such as shoes, socks, chairs, spoons, coats, hats, wellington boots and so on.
● When your child is older, try asking him, 'Pass me the *big* one, please', when you have given him a big and a small ball.

AGE RANGE
1–2 years

LEARNING OPPORTUNITIES
● To develop an understanding of 'up', 'down' and 'inside'
● To copy a sequence of actions.

YOU WILL NEED
A cardboard box; glove puppet; large pair of scissors for yourself.

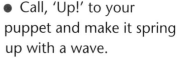

Jack-in-the-box

Sharing the game
● Start the activity by cutting off one side and the top flaps from the cardboard box.
● Fit the glove puppet on your hand and play with your toddler until she becomes used to it.
● Now tell her that Puppet is going to hide inside the box, emphasising the word 'inside'.
● Reach your arm through the open side of the box until the puppet is out of sight of your child.

● Call, 'Up!' to your puppet and make it spring up with a wave.
● Now tell the puppet to go down and lower it into the box again.
● If your child is old enough, encourage her to join in the instructions.
● Next, let your toddler take a turn at climbing into the box and working the puppet, following your instructions to 'jump *up*' or 'go *down*'.
● This game is also great fun if you ask an older brother or sister to be the puppet inside the cardboard box.

Taking it further
● Talk about 'climbing *up*' the stairs and 'going *down*' the stairs as you move about the house.
● Ask your child to hold her arms up, when you are putting on her jumper, and then to push her legs down, when you are putting trousers on her.

AGE RANGE
2–3 years

LEARNING OPPORTUNITIES
● To develop balance
● To co-operate when playing
● To develop an understanding of area.

YOU WILL NEED
A tape recorder or CD player; musical tape or CD; sheets of newspaper.

Pirates

Sharing the game

● With your child, clear a space on the floor by putting toys away and pushing back the furniture if necessary.

● Spread the sheets of newspaper out on the floor (it does not matter if they overlap), leaving some clear spaces.

● Put on some music and have a dance together, being careful not to slip.

● Stop the music and tell your child to find some newspaper to stand still on.

● Pretend that the empty floor space is the sea and each sheet of newspaper is a safe island.

● Now fold each sheet of newspaper into two and start the music again, and have another dance with him.

● Next time you stop the music, your 'islands' will be a little smaller.

● Continue the game by folding the sheets of newspaper in half, each time you stop the music, until you can no longer balance on the tiny islands!

● At the end of the game, put all your little islands together to make an island big enough for you both to stand on.

Taking it further

● Play folding games with small sheets of paper to make new shapes and paper hats.

● Cut a square piece of paper into two, then challenge your child to put the pieces together to make the square again.

AGE RANGE
2–3 years

LEARNING OPPORTUNITIES
● To explore symmetry and space
● To respond to position words.

YOU WILL NEED
A mirror on a wardrobe door, or a large plastic mirror that you can move and handle; hats and clothes to try on.

Mirror magic

Sharing the game
● If you are using a mirrored wardrobe door, start by playing together in front of it.
● Admire yourselves in the mirror, as you try on different hats and clothes, and talk about the sizes, for example, 'This is too big!' or, 'How small it is for me!'.

● Now show your child how you can hide half behind the wardrobe door and then see just part of yourself reflected in the mirror.
● If you pop just your top half and one arm out, your child will see these as well as a reflection of them, so you will look like a two-bodied, legless 'you'! Keep this funny and enjoy the patterns and body shapes that you make.
● If you use a hand-held mirror, you can make interesting reflections by placing it at different positions and angles to yourself and inviting your child to say what she can see, asking her, for example, 'How many eyes does Daddy have?' (if you are Dad).
● Take it in turns to make the body shapes, balancing and placing your bodies in different postures as you play.

Taking it further
● Angle a small plastic mirror against different shapes, pictures and patterns, and watch the symmetry. Talk about what you can see.

LEARNING OPPORTUNITIES
- To count from one to two
- To respond to 'up' and 'down'
- To copy a sequence of movements.

YOU WILL NEED
A tape or CD of 'The Grand Old Duke of York' (Traditional) and a tape recorder or CD player (all optional); drum or tambourine.

Marching up and down

Sharing the game

- Put on your tape or CD, or alternatively you can sing or chant the traditional rhyme yourself.
- Beat a drum or a tambourine as you sing or chant, to keep a strong rhythm going.
- Encourage your child to raise his arms up in the air as the Duke of York marches up the hill, and then lower them down as he marches down again:

> The Grand Old Duke of York,
> He had ten thousand men;
> He marched them up to the top of the hill,
> And he marched them down again.
> And when they were up they were up,
> And when they were down they were down,
> And when they were only half-way up,
> They were neither up nor down.
> *Traditional*

- Encourage your child to march with a strong 'one, two' rhythm, lifting his legs high and swinging his arms.

Taking it further

- Give your child a drum or a shaker to play as he marches and you chant, to the same rhythm as the third and fourth lines, 'They beat their drums to the top of the hill and they beat them down again'.
- Try playing your instruments loudly as you climb *up* the hill and softly as you come *down*.

LEARNING OPPORTUNITIES
● To link actions to 'on' and 'under'.
● To respond to time words, such as 'first', 'next' and 'last'.

YOU WILL NEED
A selection of large cardboard boxes; lightweight cover; your usual soft furniture; small toy, or sweets or dry fruit, to act as 'treasure'.

Crazy challenge

Sharing the game
● Get ready for a surprise by moving aside some furniture and making an obstacle course for your child.
● You can use all kinds of furniture already in the room, such as a table to crawl underneath, a chair to sit on top of, a cover to wriggle through, a box to climb inside, and so on.
● Show your child the room and spend some time moving around it in different ways. Talk her through what she is doing, emphasising the position words, such as 'on' and 'under'.
● Now set your child a challenge – can she first sit on the chair and next climb under the table?
● Repeat the instructions if she forgets.
● Your older child will be able to follow two or three instructions including the sequence words, 'first', 'next' and 'last'.
● Now hide the 'treasure' and tell your child where it is hidden by saying, for example, 'It's under the cloth!'. Remember to celebrate success together.

Taking it further
● Play this game with small toy animals and a toy farmyard, or with dolls' house furniture and little people, asking your child questions such as, 'Can you hide the dog *under* the bed?'.
● Look for natural opportunities throughout the day to use simple position words and sequence words, for example, when she is getting dressed and undressed.

CHAPTER 7

The games in this chapter use anticipation, imitation, sorting and matching and will help children to develop object permanence, explore how objects in their surroundings are the same or different, and develop simple concepts, such as category, shape and colour. The games are especially suitable for sitting down together so that you can support your child's play and understanding, and enjoy early learning together.

TIME TOGETHER

NOW YOU SEE IT...

In the first few months, your baby is coming to terms with the fact that objects in the world around her are stable and persist through time – this is called 'object permanence'.

Though it seems obvious to an older person, it comes as a genuine surprise to a young baby that the cat which disappeared behind the sofa should reappear again the other side. It is as if the baby forgets that it was ever there because what she cannot see ceases to exist for her. As your baby gets a little older, she is more likely to be surprised when the cat *fails to* reappear again, showing that she has now developed 'object permanence'.

How you can help
● Play repetitive 'Hide-and-seek' games such as, 'Peep-bo' and share the fun as you reappear.

● Encourage your baby to search for dropped toys.
● Hide a favourite toy beneath a scarf for her to find.
● Ask questions such as, 'Where's Mummy?' just as Mummy is about to appear around the corner.

SAME AND DIFFERENT

When your baby is little, he is busy developing his senses so that he can make sense of the world around him. In his first few weeks, he is learning to focus his eyes and to look. He can begin to 'still' or move his arms and legs more when he hears you coming. He begins to feel and mouth things that come into contact with his hands or face. Before long, he is learning that he can actively move his hands or feet in order to touch or influence other things. Through these rather random movements come purpose and intention.

His early explorations leads to the realisation that things in the world are 'different' or 'the same'. This understanding of 'same' and 'different' leads on to your baby's first understanding of simple concepts and categories, such as shape, quantity and colour.

How you can help
● Provide opportunities for your child to look and listen, talking gently as you enjoy sounds and sights together.

● Repeat sounds that you make so that your baby can begin to hear and learn similar patterns.
● Provide your child with a few familiar toys, teddies and dolls to establish sameness.
● Use your daily routines to help your child to begin to anticipate and predict, keeping events and people in his life familiar and steady.

SORTING AND MATCHING

When your child is a little older, she will appreciate that life has certain patterns and routines to it and that experiences and objects in the world can be the 'same' or 'different'. Now she is ready to begin sorting and matching. At first, this comes naturally and all you need to do is to create plenty of opportunities for your child to explore, adding your own words and commentary to help her to learn. Introducing words, such as 'same' and 'different', are an important part of early number development and are best taught by linking words to actions when your child is playing freely.

How you can help
● Keep your language very simple, emphasising the key words.
● Even toddlers will enjoy simple games in which they join in with a 'yes' or 'no' when you ask them if two things are the 'same'.
● Keep these early experiences relaxing and fun so that your child does not begin to think that there is a 'right' way and a 'wrong' way to enjoy early number games.
● Begin to provide a running commentary yourself as your child is freely playing and exploring, using simple sentences such as, 'They are both blue!', and look for any natural opportunities to use the words 'same' and 'different'.

SAME NUMBER

Two-year-olds start to use number vocabulary, such as 'same number' in their play, and to enjoy action rhymes and join in too. Three-year-olds begin to be able to look at a small set of objects, such as two ducks or three biscuits, and recognise 'two-ness' and 'three-ness' without the need to count them out. Because your child has already established object permanence, he now begins to understand that number remains constant too – if there were two teddies in the box when the lid closed, there will still be two when you open the box again.

How you can help
● Use your own language to introduce number and quantity, for example, 'Who has *the same number* now?' or, 'Can I have *a different one*?'.
● Start by keeping quantities down to under three items, until your child has grasped the idea of early counting.
● Create opportunities for your child to enjoy number rhymes and action songs, to use simple mathematical language in play and to develop an interest in numbers and counting.

CONCEPT DEVELOPMENT

Early mathematical development involves all kinds of skills and activities. These go far beyond simply learning about numbers and how to count. They include exploring shape, colour and size, and making comparisons between items. Children have to be able to distinguish between 'same' and 'different' if they are to match and sort, to group objects into categories and concepts, to notice and create patterns and sequences, and to appreciate how quantity changes.

With this understanding comes the ability to begin to form concepts and to make links in their thinking, for example, that red, blue and green are all colours, and that squares, circles and triangles are all shapes.

How you can help
● Encourage your child to show an interest in different shapes and colours by making different arrangements with toys and objects.
● Help her to see similarities in the shapes of different things in the environment and to use simple words to describe position, size and shape.
● As your child gets older, longer time will be spent in constructing and building; this is an excellent way of developing both concentration and mathematical ability.
● Above all, talk to your child about everyday experiences and her surroundings so that she has the opportunity to link abstract concept words, such as 'big', 'red' and 'square', to concrete experiences and objects.

LEARNING OPPORTUNITIES
● To look for a fallen toy
● To develop the concept of object permanence.

YOU WILL NEED
Your baby's usual chair or buggy; big cuddly toys; ribbon.

Drop and seek

Sharing the game

● Wait until your child is old enough to sit slightly upright in a rocking cradle, pushchair or high chair.
● Choose his favourite cuddly toy and make it dance about in front of him for a little while.
● Keep talking to him in a sing-song tone of voice to hold his interest.
● Now drop the cuddly toy to the floor.
● Put on an exaggerated surprised expression and exclaim, 'Where's Teddy? Gone!'. Watch your baby's expression as he tries to take in all the messages from your face and voice.
● Now look down on the floor and say, 'There's Teddy!'.
● Reach down and raise Teddy slowly up into your baby's view again, talking all the while and building up the excitement until he can see his favourite soft toy again.
● Repeat for several turns and with other toys, too.

Taking it further

● When your baby is a little older, encourage him to lean over and look with you to see where Teddy has fallen to.
● Hide Teddy under the bedclothes or under a cushion and encourage your baby to find it.

LEARNING OPPORTUNITIES
● To observe two things that are 'the same'
● To understand 'gone'.

YOU WILL NEED
A wall mirror.

AGE RANGE
0–1 year

Mirror image

Sharing the game
● Hold your baby in your arms and talk as you approach the wall mirror from the side.
● Draw your baby's attention to the mirror image by saying, 'Look! There's Mummy and (your child's name)!'.
● Younger babies will not understand that they are seeing themselves but may be struck that there are two people who look familiar!

● Hold your baby's hand gently up to the mirror so that she sees the reflection of her hand approaching. Say, 'One hand, two hands!' as you point out to her her real hand and the reflection of her hand.
● Touch the reflections of your noses in the mirror and enjoy watching your reflections change as you move about.
● Now stand to one side as you look at the mirror. Tell your baby, 'Gone!' as you both disappear out of view.
● Reappear and disappear again a few times, saying, 'Hello!' and, 'Gone!' as you play.

Taking it further
● If you add a smear of lipstick or paint to the forehead of your older baby, she will try to wipe it off from the forehead that she sees in the mirror – she is now recognising that the reflection that she sees is actually her!
● Play a game touching your hands together, your feet together and your cheeks together. This will help your baby to begin to understand the concept of 'sameness'.

LEARNING OPPORTUNITIES
● To develop awareness of 'same'
● To look and to listen.

YOU WILL NEED
Two sets of identical toys, such as two foam balls, teddy bears, baby shoes and plastic ducks; cushions or your baby's rocking cradle.

Same game

Sharing the game
● Wait until your child is old enough to enjoy handling and exploring toys to play this game.
● Sit or lie him on some cushions or in his cradle.
● Hand him one of the toys and keep the rest out of view.
● As you pass it to him, name it, for example, 'Ball'.
● Let your baby feel it, mouth it and perhaps pass it from hand to hand for a little while.
● Then hold up an identical toy, for example, the second ball, and draw his attention to both items, for example, 'Look! *Ball*! *Dad's* ball, *(your child's name)*'s ball! They're the *same*!'.
● Offer your baby the second ball to play with – he will probably drop the first one until he is a bit older.

● Repeat the game for the other toys, naming each one as you pass it to him.
● In this way, you are helping your baby to notice that the toys are the same, even though he is still too young to use the word himself.

Taking it further
● You can offer your older child a selection of toys to choose from and say to him, 'Can you find one the same?', as you show him one of the toys.

LEARNING OPPORTUNITIES
● To develop an awareness of sameness
● To be aware of body parts.

YOU WILL NEED
A comfortable armchair.

My nose, your nose

Sharing the game
● Sit down comfortably with your baby and enjoy a little cuddle or a rock together.
● When your baby is alert and interested, lead her fist to touch her nose gently.
● Say her name as you touch, for example, 'Nose! *(Your child's name)*'s nose!'.
● Draw your face close to hers and move her fist to touch your nose this time, saying, 'Nose! Mummy's nose!' (if you are Mum).
● Repeat two or three times.
● If your baby is still interested and alert, try a new body part next time and say, for example, 'Ear! *(Your child's name)*'s ear… Mummy's ear!' as you touch each ear.
● Build this up very gradually over several cuddle sessions, so that your baby becomes familiar with each body part before you introduce a new one.
● Revisit the parts that you have already practised – this is called 'consolidating' your baby's new learning – and always keep the game fun and encouraging.
● You can also play this game in front of a mirror if your child is a little older.

Taking it further
● Invite Teddy to join in too and say, for example, 'Tummy! *(Your child's name)*'s tummy, Mummy's tummy, Teddy's tummy!'.
● Invite your older baby to touch her own, yours or Teddy's nose all by herself.

LEARNING OPPORTUNITIES
● To sort into pairs
● To develop imagination
● To develop counting skills.

YOU WILL NEED
Pairs of toy animals (wooden, plastic or soft); cardboard box; large pair of scissors for yourself.

Noah's Ark

Sharing the game
● Prepare the game by making a Noah's Ark out of a cardboard box.
● Cut two slits from the top to three-quarters-way down on one side of the box and fold this panel downwards and outwards to form a wide ramp.
● Cut windows for the animals in the other sides of the box.
● Now encourage your toddler to watch and join in as you pair all the animals up together and march them two by two into the ark.
● Make the ark go for a sail around the floor as the animals look out of the windows.
● Stop at an island and encourage your toddler to help all the animals to come out to play.
● When it is time for them to go back into the ark, ask your toddler to help to find each pair.
● He might enjoy it if you call the animals by their names, for example, *Jo* Duck and *Jenny* Duck, or *Mr* Duck and *Mrs* Duck.

Taking it further
● Make a simple game of 'Pairs' by cutting out the fronts of identical greetings cards and helping your toddler to match them in pairs.
● Use more cardboard boxes to make homes for pairs of animals.

AGE RANGE
1–2 years

LEARNING OPPORTUNITIES
● To identify things that roll
● To develop an awareness of round shapes.

YOU WILL NEED
An incline – indoors or outdoors – or a tray or board to make one; selection of items that roll, such as balls, cylinders, empty round containers and wheeled toys; selection of items that do not roll, such as boxes, teddy bears, clothing, plastic toys and so on; basket or box.

Does it roll?

Sharing the game
● If you do not have an incline, make one by resting one end of a large tray or board on to the bottom indoor stair or outdoor step.
● Look for the kind of slope that is just steep enough to allow round objects to roll, but just shallow enough to allow the other things to get stuck.
● Have fun together collecting all the items into a box or basket and carry it over to the slope.
● Take an item from the basket and place it at the top of the slope.
● Watch to see if it rolls or gets stuck.
● Have turns with the other items and see what happens each time.
● After a while, offer your toddler turns and ask her questions such as, 'Can you find something that *rolls*?'.
● See if she takes the round items out of the basket or box. You can

pretend to be unlucky and choose the square-shaped ones!
● Clap and cheer when your toddler finds something that rolls right down the slope.
● See whose item rolls the furthest.

Taking it further
● Talk together about the shapes that roll and introduce the word 'round' in your conversation.
● Next time you play, see if she can chose some things that she thinks will be good to roll.

AGE RANGE
1–2 years

LEARNING OPPORTUNITIES
● To develop understanding of 'gone' and 'under'
● To develop curiosity
● To identify 'same' and 'different' by touch.

YOU WILL NEED
A sand-pit outdoors, or a box of paper shavings (or similar) indoors; sheets of newspaper, or a plastic sheet to protect your indoor floor if necessary; pairs of identical toys, such as animals, play people, cars and so on.

THINK FIRST!
Make sure that outdoor sand-pits are kept covered to prevent animals from using them.

Bury and find

Sharing the game
● Prepare for this game by burying the sets of identical toys in the sand-pit or 'bran tub' (your box of shavings) with your toddler.
● As each toy disappears from sight, say, for example, 'Gone! It's *under* the sand!'.
● Next, show your toddler what to do. Dip your arm into the shavings or sand and feel around until you find something solid.

● Then think about what it might be, saying, for example, 'It's hard, it's got wheels… Is it a tractor?'.
● Lift the object out of the sand and discover whether you were right.
● Now see if you can find another object that is 'just the same' with your toddler. Reach in for a feel and say, for example, 'Has this got wheels? No… Has this got wheels?… Yes!'.
● Continue until you have managed to find all the pairs of toys.
● Each time you find a pair, hold both toys up together and celebrate, exclaiming, for example, 'Yes! They're the *same*!'.

Taking it further
● Wrap small presents up and bury them in a bran tub for children to find as a party game.
● Ask your older child if he can feel for a toy that is 'the same' or one that is 'different'.

LEARNING OPPORTUNITIES
● To practise simple sorting
● To develop imagination.

YOU WILL NEED
A set of farmyard animals; large sheet of paper; empty cardboard boxes and containers; washable felt-tipped pens; scissors for yourself.

Farmyards

Sharing the game

● This is a very simple game, but a real favourite for learning to sort and to match.

● Make a simple farmyard by cutting into boxes and containers to make sheds and houses.

● Arrange these on the large sheet of paper, then draw in fences and colour in fields with your toddler, who will probably be happy to help. She can colour the fields over in a rough scribble while you ink in the boundaries of the fields and yards, for example.

● Now have fun arranging the animals in the farm. Start with all the pigs in one field, all the cows in another, all the hens in the yard, all the ducks on the pond, and so on.

● Continue to play and enjoy the game together, talking to your toddler and encouraging her imaginative play.

● At the end of the game, sort the animals once more into their different fields, sheds or yards, and say 'good-night' to the animals.

Taking it further

● On a sunny day, create a miniature farmyard out of doors with boxes and larger toys and invite your toddler to explore the farm with her whole body.

● Try to spot the farm animals when you are out and about on a journey, commenting as you go, for example, 'There's a field with *cows* in… And there's one full of *sheep*!'.

LEARNING OPPORTUNITIES
● To sort by colour and size
● To develop early counting skills
● To talk about 'more' and 'less'.

YOU WILL NEED
A collection of approximately 30 large buttons; empty biscuit-selection tin, complete with plastic inset; pot.

THINK FIRST!
Take care that your child does not swallow small buttons.

Button pot

Sharing the game
● Collect old buttons from jumble sales or clothing that you are recycling. Chunky coat and cardigan buttons are excellent. You will need several of each kind for this game.

● Place all the buttons in a pot, well out of the way until you are ready to play.
● Look out for a suitable biscuit tin that has a plastic inset divided into different spaces for each kind of biscuit.
● Sit at a table with your child and show him the button collection.
● Enjoy playing with the buttons for a while and see if your child notices that some of them are 'the same'.
● Then suggest that you see if there are any other buttons that are the same, too.
● Show him how to use the sections in the biscuit tin to sort the different buttons into.
● Next, count the buttons in each space together.
● Finally, see which space has 'more' or 'less' buttons in it.

Taking it further
● Challenge your child to try sorting out the buttons in different ways, for example, sorting black buttons from blue buttons, the bigger ones from the smaller ones, or the buttons with two holes from the ones with four.
● Challenge your child to give you two buttons, three red buttons and so on.

LEARNING OPPORTUNITIES
● To sort into same pairs
● To develop imagination.

YOU WILL NEED
All your soft toys; tape recorder, CD player or video recorder and television; music on a tape, CD, video or television; small biscuits or snacks.

Toyland parade

Sharing the game
● Make a space on the floor and bring out all the soft toys.
● Play with them for a while and enjoy greeting some old friends!
● Now tell your child that each toy wants to find a friend. Ask her to choose one of the toys and then to try to find a friend for it, such as someone who is the same in some way.
● This will give you plenty of opportunity to talk about 'the same' and 'different'. For example, Pink Ted wants to go with Pink Panther because they are both the same colour, or Nelly Elephant wants to go with Bert Elephant because they are both elephants.
● As you pair up the toys, line them up for a big parade.
● Play some music or sing a song at the end for the toys' big parade.
● Now mix all the toys together for a party! Share out the biscuits or snacks, making sure that all the toys have the same amount.

Taking it further
● Your older child will be able to work out how each toy can find a friend who is different in some way.
● Choose two toys and talk about the things that are the same between them, and those that are different. Keep your language short and simple.

Puppet pranks

TIME TOGETHER

AGE RANGE
2–3 years

LEARNING OPPORTUNITIES
● To count to three
● To respond to 'same number'.

YOU WILL NEED
A glove puppet; nine healthy snacks or biscuits; three plastic plates.

Sharing the game

● Introduce the glove puppet and make it behave in a friendly way to your child. Tell each other your names.
● Pretend that the puppet, called 'Happy', has come to play and explain that he would like to stay for tea.
● Tell your child to go and fetch three plates and the snack that you have left out for him. Help him to count out the plates.
● Place the plates out on the table, one in front of you, your child and Happy.

● Now make Happy become very excited and say that he wants to share out the snacks between you!
● Make a big show of Happy picking up one snack at a time and placing it on a plate. Make him count, 'One for you, one for you… two for me!'.
● As this goes on, ask your child if he thinks that it is fair! Count the snacks together and encourage your child to tell you who has more and who has less.
● Let Happy have another go, but let him still make mistakes.
● Now encourage your child to help to put the count right, asking him, 'How can you share out the snacks fairly?'.
● Enjoy your snacks together!

Taking it further

● Share out snacks between your child's soft toys. Count to see if they all have the same amount.

LEARNING OPPORTUNITIES
● To name simple shapes
● To explore and stick with shapes.

YOU WILL NEED
Clean paper plates, bowls and cups; square-edged packets and boxes; sheets of A3 cardboard; glue; different-shaped stickers; scissors for yourself; plastic sheet.

Squares and circles

Sharing the game
● Start by cutting one sheet of A3 cardboard into the largest square that it will make, and another into a circle.
● Arrange the card shapes, glue and materials on to a table covered with a plastic sheet.
● Sit down with your child and talk about the two card shapes that you have made.
● Encourage her to feel the round edge of the circle and introduce the words 'round' and 'circle'.
● Now show her the square and feel the corners, introducing the words 'straight' and 'square'.
● Now work together with your child as you make a 'round' collage and a 'square' one.
● On to the round card, stick and mount the round shapes of the paper plates, bowls and cups as well as round stickers.

● On to the square card, stick square-edged cardboard packages and square stickers.
● Each time you find a new piece, feel along the shape's edge to see if it is 'round' or 'straight'.

Taking it further
● Make a collage out of different-shaped pieces of coloured paper, such as circles, squares and triangles.
● Look for round shapes around your home and see how many you can count together, for example, the face of a clock, the top of a waste-paper basket and so on.

CHAPTER 8

Sleep comes more naturally when children feel tired, settled, confident and secure, and an excellent way to achieve this is through a regular and relaxing routine. In this chapter, you will find games for quiet times, before rest time and for the end of the day, to help your child to think about daily routines, wind down with you and feel calm, relaxed, settled and confident after a busy time.

WINDING DOWN

FOLLOWING ROUTINES

Understanding sequences is an important part of learning about numbers. One of the first sequences that your baby will understand is the sequences of time, and this will come naturally as you take him through predictable daily routines. New babies follow their own routines rather than yours. They wake and sleep according to the signals from their own bodies – when they feel tired, when they are uncomfortable, when they are hungry, when they are full and so on. Your baby has been born with the instinct to cry when he needs something and this is his way of communicating with you.

Experts used to think that we should impose routines on babies right from the early days, but we now know that we should read the messages that a new baby is giving us and respond to them on demand. This is all part of forming the warm relationship between you and your baby, which will help him to develop into a more settled and confident child. When he is a few months older, he will be able to choose, to a certain extent, whether he wakes or sleeps, and routines become a natural and important part of family life. Toddlers can sometimes negotiate and push boundaries to their limits if there is no routine or pattern to the day.

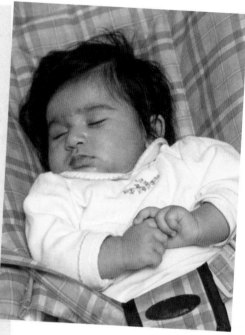

How you can help

● Try to be relaxed in the early stages and listen to the messages that your baby is giving you when he needs feeding, changing or playing with.
● When you see a pattern to his sleeping and feeding beginning to emerge, you can begin to shape this into a regular routine.
● By his first birthday, try to have a regular winding-down and settling routine for bedtime and rest time.
● Avoid energetic play or games before bed – and make sure that any partner or colleagues apply this rule too!
● Try to give five minutes of unconditional time to settle your child in bed and share stories and talk just before sleep.

SEQUENCES OF TIME
It will take a while for your child to be able to understand sequences of time, that is, what usually happens after what. The first thing that she

will understand is that when she is hungry, you will come to her and you will do something about it. You may begin to notice her distress increasing as you approach (because she is so hungry) or her distress decreasing (because she knows that she is about to be fed) – both are typical reactions and you should not worry that she reacts in one way more than the other.

Between one and two, your toddler will be making links between what she does and the effect that it has on others. This is where routines can really help – if she learns that shouting loud enough always brings you back after bedtime, it could develop into a game of its own. Routines help your child to understand the passage of time. They also help her to learn that one thing inevitably leads to another, to begin to anticipate what will happen next and to feel secure. That is why many of the games in this book involve anticipation.

How you can help
● Use the same tone of voice or greeting as you approach your baby.
● Build in little rituals to your daily life, such as a bathtime song, settling the

teddies into bed, an order for putting on coats, shoes and hats when you go out, a 'click' of the seat belt in the car, and so on.
● Make the best use of routines as they give your child a warning of what will happen next – for example, teatime leads to bathtime leads to story time leads to bedtime.
● Use photographs to talk about what happened in the past and to discuss what will happen in the future, such as going on holiday or going on an outing.
● Try to always give warnings of what will happen next, for example, 'After your video it will be time to eat'.

FEELING CONFIDENT
Confidence grows from having a warm and secure relationship with the adults around you. We now know that some of the best ways of forming this relationship are to tune into what your baby is trying to tell you, and to share pleasure and fun together. That is why a game-like approach is so useful in helping your child to develop and learn. When he is older, confidence will also grow if he knows clearly what is expected of him, if he feels successful in what he does and he is offered choices whenever this is appropriate. By using games, you can encourage your child to feel successful with numbers and to see them as fun and not just 'work'.

How you can help
● Be aware of days when you may be feeling particularly stressed. These are the days when it can help to have some

simple number games and activities up your sleeve.
● When you are playing number games with your child, try to enjoy the process. The main aim is for you to enjoy your time together, so if a game is not working, simply stop it and do something else.
● Try not to give the impression that there is a right way and a wrong way of playing with numbers, and always make your child feel successful.

RELAXING AND WINDING DOWN
Bedtimes can be particularly difficult for your young child since this is the time when she has to separate from you and fall asleep on her own. That is why this chapter has many games, rituals and routines that will help her to feel relaxed and confident at the end of the day or before rest time. Your aim is to reduce the level of excitement and physical activity, so that she does not struggle against sleep and drifts easily into her dreams. Unfortunately, bedtime battles with one- and two-year-olds can make this difficult and leave everyone feeling more aroused and unsettled. A calm, regular routine will help to overcome these problems.

How you can help
● Try to match your bedtime or rest-time routine to the age and stage that your child has reached.
● If you are at home and have more than one child, try to stagger bedtimes so that you can spend individual time with each of the children, and enjoy some of these suggested games together.
● The last number and shape games that you play in the day need to be undemanding and leave your child feeling successful and appreciated, as well as relaxed and settled.

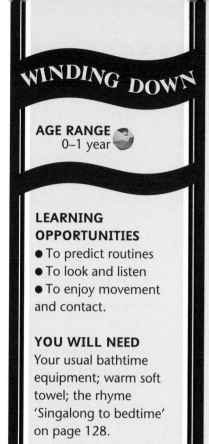
LEARNING OPPORTUNITIES
- To predict routines
- To look and listen
- To enjoy movement and contact.

YOU WILL NEED
Your usual bathtime equipment; warm soft towel; the rhyme 'Singalong to bedtime' on page 128.

Singalong

Sharing the game

- Although this game is best suited for babies at home, you can adapt it for washing and rest-time routines in a setting, if appropriate.
- Chant the rhyme softly, or sing it to the tune of 'Twinkle, Twinkle, Little Star' (Traditional).
- Start to sing the first verse of the song as you carry your baby to the bathroom. When he is a little older, the song will become a signal that the familiar routine is about to begin.
- Sing the first verse again as you take off his clothes and prepare him for the bath.
- Repeat once more as you support his head and splash the water gently over his body.
- The next verse signals that it is time to be dried. Sing it as you wrap your baby warmly in the towel and make this a special time together to enjoy a cuddle.
- As you carry him to his cot, sing the last verse softly.
- Make your voice softer and softer as you give a final kiss and gentle stroke to say 'good-night'.

Taking it further

- Plan a regular routine for bedtime or rest time so that your baby can start to predict that one thing leads inevitably and calmly to the next. This will help him to understand daily routines and time sequences. Avoid lively play or games just when you are helping him to wind down.

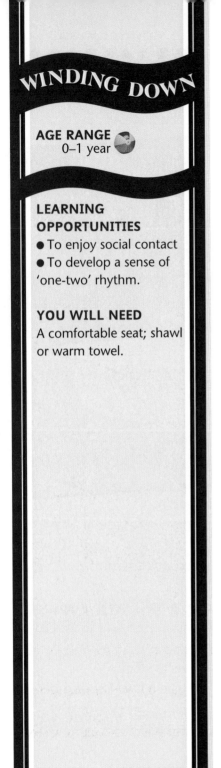

LEARNING OPPORTUNITIES
● To enjoy social contact
● To develop a sense of 'one-two' rhythm.

YOU WILL NEED
A comfortable seat; shawl or warm towel.

Rocking time

Sharing the game

● This is a relaxing number rhyme that you can share before rest time, when you are drying your baby after bathtime or a feed.

● Wrap her up warmly and cosily, sit in a comfortable chair and hold her in your arms.

● Watch your baby's face and try to hold her eye contact as you gently rock her first one way and then the other.

● Chant this rhyme slowly as you rock, moving to the rhythm:

One, two, I love you
Three, four, Tell me more
Five, six, You're the best
Seven, eight, Think you're great!
Nine, ten, Start again…
Hannah Mortimer

● Use it as an excuse for plenty of cuddles!

● Repeat the rhyme two or three times, then change the last line to:

Nine, ten, That's the end!

Taking it further

● Introduce more traditional rhymes and songs to your baby that have 'one-two' rhythms. For example, 'Cobbler, Cobbler, Mend my Shoe, get it done by half past two' and 'Row, Row, Row Your Boat'.

LEARNING OPPORTUNITIES
● To develop awareness of rolling
● To anticipate a sequence
● To enjoy physical contact.

YOU WILL NEED
A rug, towel or cot duvet.

This way, that way

Sharing the game
● Spread the rug, towel or duvet on the floor for your baby to lie on.
● Lie your baby on his back and kneel over him so that your face is close to his.
● Gently roll him to one side as you sing this song very slowly, to the tune of 'Row, Row, Row Your Boat' (Traditional).

Roll, roll, roll along
Rolling to and fro,
First go one way,
     then come back
Rolling as you go.
Hannah Mortimer

● Tuck your baby's right arm down by his side and gently bring his left arm over as you roll him to his right. Then gently return him to his back.
● Now tuck his left arm down by his side and gently bring his right arm over as you roll him to his left.
● With your older baby, start the roll and let him finish it as he wiggles quickly on to his tummy – he is now able to anticipate.
● When he reaches this stage, you can roll him right over one way, and then right over back again.
● Sing the song as you play and keep the game fun so that he relaxes and begins to predict the next movement.

Taking it further
● Start your baby on his tummy and roll him over on his back.
● Place toys just out of reach and encourage your baby to roll towards them.

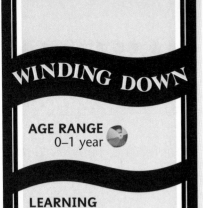

WINDING DOWN

AGE RANGE
0–1 year

LEARNING OPPORTUNITIES
● To anticipate
● To develop an awareness of a circular movement
● To look and to listen.

YOU WILL NEED
Somewhere quiet to sit comfortably.

The merry-go-round

Sharing the game
● The traditional rhyme 'Round and Round the Garden' is ideal for teaching your baby how to anticipate what comes next and for sharing fun together.
● Sit your baby down on your knee.
● Hold one of her hands in yours and use the forefinger of your other hand to trace a circular movement in her palm.
● Chant this rhyme as you move your finger around, substituting your child's name for 'Molly':

Round and round the merry-go-round
Go Molly and her Mummy –
One step, two steps,
Tickle her on the tummy!
Hannah Mortimer

● On the third line, make your fingers walk up your baby's arms, ending with a gentle tickle of her tummy.
● Now repeat on the other palm.
● Watch your baby's eyes – you will notice her begin to smile and wiggle her hand away when she is a little older. This means that she is anticipating what is going to happen next.
● Try some variations – for example, trace a 'round and round' pattern on her tummy for the first two lines, ending with a gentle tickle under her chin.
● Now make a circular movement on your baby's back. Can she still anticipate what will happen at the end? If so, this means that she is making links between her sense of touch and her thinking.

Taking it further
● Teach your older child to begin to do the actions back to you.
● Practise 'round and round' scribbles with your fingers on a misted mirror or on a wet table-top, saying, 'Round and round' as you do.

LEARNING OPPORTUNITIES
● To develop early counting
● To recognise numerals
● To look and to listen.

YOU WILL NEED
A blank exercise book or scrap book; broad felt-tipped pen for yourself; bold stickers.

Story time

Sharing the game
● Select picture stickers that your child will be interested in and that come in sets so that there are two or three of the identical picture.
● You will need to prepare for this game by making a simple story-book, using a blank exercise book and the stickers.
● Examine your stickers and think of a very simple story that you could build around six of them. Here is an example:
One day *a teddy bear* went for a walk to the zoo. He saw *two tigers*. Then he saw *three elephants*. He said 'hello' to *one lion*. He ran away from *two snakes*. And he was very surprised to see *three dinosaurs*! Goodbye, *Teddy Bear*!
● Keep your story very simple.
● Write one sentence on each page of the exercise book in bold print and leave a page next to it for an illustration of the teddy bear, two tigers and so on.
● In this example, the first illustration will be a teddy-bear sticker. Write a bold number '1' underneath.
● Then you will have illustrations of two tigers, three elephants, one lion, two snakes, three dinosaurs and finally one teddy bear to say 'goodbye' to. Each will have its number written underneath.

● Sit down together to enjoy the story, stopping on each illustration to touch and count the number of stickers together.
● Hold your toddler's finger and use it to trace gently over each written number as you say it together.

Taking it further
● Your older child will be able to cope with a slightly longer story and with counting up to five.

AGE RANGE
1–2 years

LEARNING OPPORTUNITIES
● To develop early counting
● To become familiar with numerals
● To relax at bedtime or rest time.

YOU WILL NEED
A plastic coat-hanger; hook or somewhere to hang it from; cardboard; foil; glue; different-coloured glitter; thread; scissors for yourself.

Starlight mobile

Sharing the game
● Prepare for this game by making a star mobile to hang near to your toddler's cot or bed.
● First, cut out five star shapes from the cardboard, each about 10cm across.
● Make a small hole in one point in each star shape and put some thread through it. Leave a good length of thread attached to the stars, but make sure that they are all different lengths.
● Tear some foil and wrap it carefully around each star shape so that both sides are covered with reflective silver.
● Now use the glue to make a bold number '1' on one side of the first star, '2' on the second, and so on until '5' for the fifth.
● Use different-coloured glitter for each star and sprinkle it on thickly to form a glittery number.
● Leave to dry, then gently number the other side of each star with the same numbers.

● When the shapes are completely dry, shake off any loose glitter and suspend each star from the coat-hanger's rail, with the number '1' hanging lowest and the number '5' highest.
● Find somewhere to hang it where the glitter will not bother you.
● Each bedtime or rest time, watch the mobile with your child and point out the numbers to her as you say them together.

Taking it further
● Your older child will enjoy helping you to make the mobile.
● Use coloured pens or cut out sticky paper numbers for a simpler version if you prefer not to use glitter.

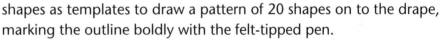

WINDING DOWN

AGE RANGE
1–2 years

LEARNING OPPORTUNITIES
● To identify and match shapes
● To respond to the names of shapes.

YOU WILL NEED
A dark drape to hang across your child's bedroom or your rest-room window, with a simple method of holding it in place (such as elastic loops on to each end of the curtain rail); non-toxic fabric glue; paper; broad felt-tipped marker pen and scissors for yourself; remnants of heavy fabrics and materials.

Shadow stick

Sharing the game
● Summer bedtimes and rest times can be more problematic than winter ones because the days are longer. Here is an idea for making the bedroom or rest room darker in a way that your child should find acceptable and fun.

● Prepare for this activity by making a drape to fit the bedroom or rest-room window.
● On the paper, make four shapes (a square, circle, triangle and star), each approximately 10cm across, and cut them out.
● Lay the drape flat on a table and use the paper shapes as templates to draw a pattern of 20 shapes on to the drape, marking the outline boldly with the felt-tipped pen.
● Then use the same templates to make 20 matching shapes in different fabrics and cut them out.
● Invite your child to help you to match the fabric shapes to their 'shadows' on the drape, naming them for him as you play.
● Use trial and error and constant encouragement to keep this game successful, until all the shapes are matched.
● Stick the pieces of fabric into place together with glue.
● When the shapes are dry and it is bedtime, hang the drape ceremoniously in place and enjoy it before you draw the curtains across it.
● You should now have a darkened room ready for sleep!

Taking it further
● Play a similar game with sheets of paper and sticky paper shapes.

LEARNING OPPORTUNITIES
● To settle down at rest time
● To develop an understanding of 'under' and 'over'.

YOU WILL NEED
Your usual rest place or bedroom, cuddly toys and bed covers.

Under cover

Sharing the game

● Wait until it is rest time or bedtime.
● Tuck your child up and make sure that all her favourite cuddly toys are lying next to her.
● Take her favourite cuddly toy and act out this settling-down rhyme with it:

Panda go over, Panda go under
Cuddling down for a snooze with Alex.
Alex go under, Alex go over
Sleep happily dreamily sleepily.
Sleep.

Hannah Mortimer

● On the first line, substitute the name of the toy. Place it gently over the covers, then tuck it under the bedclothes.

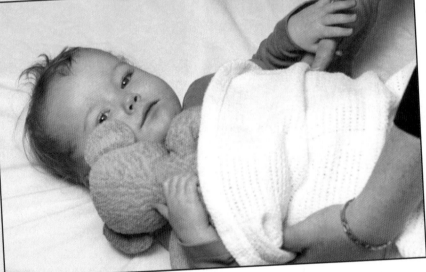

● On the second line, substitute the name of your child – it does not matter if it does not scan.
● Slow the chant right down as you say the last two lines, softening your voice as well.
● Lift the covers gently above your child's head, then tuck them back into place on the third line and straighten the bedclothes.
● End with a whisper and a kiss.

● This will not always send your child to sleep, but when used as part of your regular routine, it will help her to relax and snuggle more happily into bed.

Taking it further

● Play a game with the cuddly toys hiding 'under' the bedclothes or jumping 'over' the pillows when you wake up.

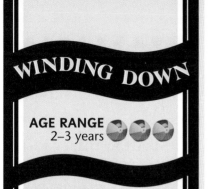
LEARNING OPPORTUNITIES
● To respond to position and size words
● To enjoy playing imaginatively.

YOU WILL NEED
Cardboard boxes; scissors for yourself; selection of soft toys and covers.

Beds for my toys

Sharing the game
● If you are at home, you can play this game in your child's bedroom once he is changed, bathed and ready for bed.
● Prepare for it together earlier in the day. Suggest to your child that you make some beds for the soft toys. Use his ideas and your sharp scissors to cut different-sized beds out of the cardboard boxes.

● As you play, encourage your child to match big toys to the bigger beds and small toys to the smaller beds.
● Cut or select covers to go on the beds, again encouraging your child to work out which size of cover will go with which bed.
● You can also look for small toys to act as cuddly toys for the larger ones!
● As you play, use words to describe the sizes of the beds and covers, such as, 'big', 'small', 'too big', 'too small', 'smaller' and 'bigger'.
● Also use position words to describe what you are doing with the toys, beds and covers, for example, 'under', 'over', 'on top', 'underneath', 'beside' and so on.
● Carry everything to your child's bedroom at bedtime or rest time.
● Stand back as he sorts out the toys, their beds and their covers.
● Make a ceremony of saying 'good-night' to the toys together before you tuck your child in.

Taking it further
● Use boxes and props to act out 'Goldilocks and the Three Bears' (Traditional), encouraging your child to match bears, bowls, chairs and beds.

 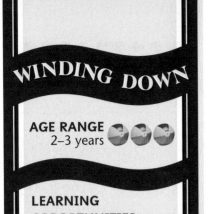
LEARNING OPPORTUNITIES
● To explore symmetry
● To trace numbers
● To match colours and shapes.

YOU WILL NEED
Five sheets of coloured A4 paper; scissors for yourself; coloured felt-tipped pens; selection of shape stickers; tray.

Butterfly wings

Sharing the game

● Prepare for this game by making five paper butterfly shapes, each a different colour.

● Do this by folding each sheet of paper into two and drawing half a butterfly shape on to one side, with the half-body on the fold, then cutting around the body and wings.

● Write a clear number '1' on the body of the first shape, '2' on the second, and so on up to '5' on the fifth.

● Put the shapes on a tray with the stickers, and wait until you want a quiet game to play together before bedtime or rest time.

● Sit down together on a sofa with the tray on your knees.

● Show your child the first butterfly. Let her choose one sticker to stick on to one wing. Whatever she chooses, you must choose an identical sticker to place in the same position on the second wing, making a mirror image.

● Count the '1' together on each wing and trace the number '1' on the body with your fingers.

● Continue by encouraging your child to stick two stickers on one of the wings of the second butterfly, then matching them symmetrically on to the second wing, counting them as you go.

● Do this for the rest of the butterflies, until you have five shape stickers on each wing of the fifth one.

● Keep the game successful by not making too many demands on your child and by counting with her (and for her) if necessary.

Taking it further

● When your child is older or more alert, she will be able to place the stickers on the second wings to match those that you have stuck on the first ones.

AGE RANGE
2–3 years

LEARNING OPPORTUNITIES
● To enjoy number rhymes
● To get ready for bed or rest time.

YOU WILL NEED
Special stickers and poster.

The pyjama rhyme

Sharing the game
● Bedtimes can sometimes become battlegrounds if you do not follow a regular routine and keep it fun. This is an idea for making a game of them.
● As you get your child ready for bed, make a point of counting his arms and his legs as he lifts them out of trousers or sleeves.
● Provide just as much help as he seems to need, letting him do it all himself if he is ready to, while you chant this rhyme:

> Time to put pyjamas on, it's nearly time for bed
> *One* arm up, *two* arms up, and pull them past your head
> *One* leg, *two* legs, pull your trousers high
> Give a twirl and take a bow, now off to bed you fly!
> *Hannah Mortimer*

● You can change the last line to fit in with your particular routine, for example:

> Give a twirl and take a bow, and down the stairs you fly!

● You can also adapt the rhyme for changing time:

> Time to put your trousers on, it's nearly time for play!

● Even when your child is dressing himself, stay close to applaud and encourage him so that he does not feel that becoming independent has deprived him of your company.
● Stickers can sometimes work well for those occasions when he puts on his pyjamas all by himself. Make a special poster for them and count them together each time you add one.

Taking it further
● Enjoy the action song 'Bananas in Pyjamas' by Carey Blyton in *Apusskidu* chosen by Beatrice Harrop (A & C Black).

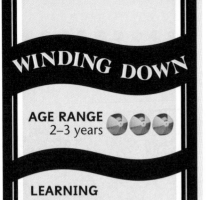
AGE RANGE
2–3 years

LEARNING OPPORTUNITIES
● To settle down after a busy time
● To count to three
● To understand the sequence words 'first', 'next' and 'last'.

YOU WILL NEED
Large floor cushions or beanbags to snuggle into; selection of picture books.

All is calm

Sharing the game
● Arrange a suitable selection of picture books in your child's bedroom or in your book area. Select stories that are not too long and that are your child's favourites.
● Be prepared for her to choose the same one again and again, and do not let any impatience show – this is your child's 'unconditional' time with you!
● Encourage her to choose three story-books, helping her to count them if necessary.

● Bring the books to the cushions and spend a few minutes quietly enjoying the first one together.
● Ask your child to put it back on the shelf and to tell you how many books there are left now.
● Repeat for the next story, so that there is just one left.
● When you have looked through all three books, talk quietly about the 'first' book, the 'next' book and the 'last' book. See if you can remember what you read together.

Taking it further
● Enjoy a regular visit to the local library and choose good bedtime stories for home.
● Invite your child to help you to put away the books on the floor, but to leave just three stories out for you both to read.

NUMBER RHYMES

The rhymes on the following pages provide lively new ways of introducing early number skills. Use them to add some fun to your daily routines such as getting up, washing hands and preparing for bedtime.

Good morning, sunshine!

Wake up little sleepy head,
Shake away your sleep!
Come over to the window
And take a little peep.
The sunshine is awake now
Come closer and you'll see;
It's time to leave your bed now
With a one – two – three!

Hannah Mortimer

Starting the day

Peep through the curtains and what do you see?
I see the sun and the sun sees me
With a yawn and a stretch and a three, two, one
Jump out of bed and let's have some fun!

Hannah Mortimer

USING THE RHYMES

Enjoy these rhymes together as you greet the new day. Slow down as you count, and end with a lift or a jump out of bed! (See the game 'Good morning!' on page 20 for more ideas.)

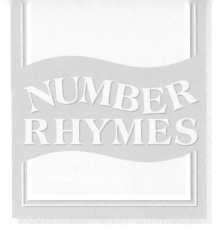

Dandy handy

One little, two little hands need washing;
Hold them in the water and make them wet!
One, two, three, four, five little fingers
Rub them and scrub them and don't forget!
One, two, three, four, five more fingers
The dirtiest fingers you've ever seen!
Wash them and dry them and look at the difference –
Ten little fingers smart and clean!

Hannah Mortimer

USING THE RHYME

Use this counting rhyme as you wash hands together with your child. Take it slowly so that you have time to touch and count each finger in turn. (See the game 'Dirty… clean!' on page 30 for more ideas.)

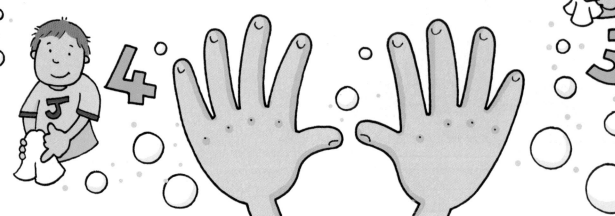

NUMBER RHYMES

Two little dicky birds

Two little dicky birds sitting on a wall,
One named Peter, one named Paul;
Fly away Peter, fly away Paul;
Come back, Peter, come back, Paul!

Traditional

Two little jellyfish

Two little jellyfish swimming in the sea,
One named Darren, one named Lee;
Swim away, Darren, swim away, Lee;
Come back Darren, come back, Lee!

Hannah Mortimer

Two little butterflies

Two little butterflies fluttering around
One on a flower, one on the ground;
Flutter by butterfly, flutter by home;
Better flutter butterfly, flutter by home!

Hannah Mortimer

USING THE RHYMES

Enjoy these action rhymes with your child and make your fingers or hands disappear and reappear again as you say the lines. In 'Two little butterflies', make your fingers gently flutter around your child, then flutter them behind your back as they disappear 'home'. (See the game 'Two little dicky birds' on page 58 for more ideas.)

Singalong to bedtime

Now it's time to have a bath,
Wash your arms and have a splash.
Unpeel baby, three two one,
Into the water when you're done!
Now it's time to have a bath,
Wash your arms and have a splash.

Now it's time to come to me,
Wrap you warm as warm can be.
Dry your fingers, dry your toes,
Here comes nappy – on it goes!
Now it's time to come to me
Wrap you warm as warm can be.

Now it's time to go to bed,
Time for bye-byes, sleepy head.
Here's a cuddle, say good-night,
See you in the morning light.
Now it's time to go to bed,
Time for bye-byes, sleepy head.

Hannah Mortimer

USING THE RHYME

Start to sing the first verse as you get
ready for bathtime, to let your baby
know what is going to happen next.
Sing the second verse as you have a
cuddle and dry your baby. Sing the
last verse softly and slowly as you kiss
'good-night'. (See the game
'Singalong' on page 113 for more
ideas.)

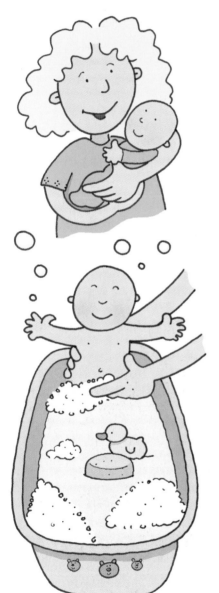